21-Day Spending Detox: Reset to Gain and Maintain Financial Freedom

by

Charity A. Morris

21-DAY SPENDING DETOX

Reset to Gain and Maintain Financial Freedom

CHARITY A. MORRIS

21-Day Spending Detox:
Reset to Gain and Maintain Financial Freedom
Copyright 2022 © Charity A. Morris

Scribe Publications

Published by
Scribe Publications, Inc.
609-961-1755
www.scribepublicationsinc.com

ISBN-13: 979-8-9853854-2-7

Library of Congress Control Number: 2022914943

Printed in the United States of America

Dedication

This book is dedicated to my husband, Gary Morris. The countless hours of conversations, the challenges, the combats, the care, and the caress got us to a better place. I love doing life with you. I am forever grateful.

Acknowledgements

Above all, Jesus, I thank You for grace beyond measure! Through all my shortcomings, victories and opportunities to learn and grow, You continue to give me persistent patience, unfailing love, and merciful provision.

To my master negotiator, Hebron, and my spicy firecracker, Hannah the Boss Baby… you are two of my WHYs. I push and persevere because I know the world will be a better place from your influence. Keep shining and excelling my beautiful babies. Your future is bright.

To my money mentors in my head, Janai Thornton and Dave Ramsey, I have listened to your programs over the years and have applied your wisdom. IT REALLY WORKS!

To three of the ones who have opened my eyes to the limitless world of financial independence: Thaxter Arteberry, Dotch Phillips and Veronica Moore. Our countless conversations were part of the inspiration to get me where I am today. Thank you for challenging me to do my best and be my best.

Table of Contents

FOREWORD

As an investment strategist and behavioral economist at Decimalytics, I notice individuals, not just in households but also many small business owners we serve, irrationally spend without regard for their finances to fill a void. I also notice the same individuals complain about lacking support to meet financial obligations. I see the same behavior in highly functional, successful people I work with globally. Quite often, many are not aware of the lack of financial responsibility practiced daily, which leads to the conversation within this book.

Although I have an academic and professional background in finance, I, too, was a victim of poor financial management at some point. Like many, I was consumed with the here and now instead of the outcome of my decisions. I later learned that I am not the only one who falls victim to late notices and indecisive budgets while looking good on the outside, knowing my daily financial decisions were tearing up the truth about myself.

Managing household finances is hard, even for people who know exactly what to do. The proof is in the pudding; as I learned, in 2022, consumer spending reached an all-time high of $13916.87 billion. We often wonder why individuals are significantly evolving more into consumers instead of producers. The thought behind this behavior is that individuals, including relatively successful people, place more value on material possessions and the connection between satisfaction and normal goods.

The first step to addressing individuals disconnect with their money is to examine the difference between needs and wants while tracking their spending to acknowledge the why behind the behavior.

First, one concedes that wealth is emphasized the most regardless of socioeconomic class. Wealth is identified by the total of tangible and intangible assets one acquires over time. What many are not taught is that wealth will include liabilities.

How did society become a place where debt is highly noted across the United States? Quickly, most were taught to live the American Dream regardless of how much it may impact their finances. From youth, parents teach their children to get an education, work at a job until retirement, buy a large house, and buy a luxury vehicle. The least expected conversation concerns proper money management and how tangible items may connect to emotional spending.

Charity Morris's book is a treasure of financial possibilities for growth. Such a book was a long time coming, given that many spend more than we earn. This book is a gem to emphasize how we need to detox from spending to acknowledge our faults and take control of our finances.

Bahiyah Shabazz, MBA, Doctoral Candidate
Investment Strategist. Economist. Author. Speaker.
Founder of Decimalytics and Brown Girls Do Invest

PREFACE

It's time for you to control-alt-delete your money mindset.

It's time to turn on yourself to help yourself.

It's time to take ownership of where you are.

IT'S TIME TO FACE YOUR FINANCES.

Are your finances all over the place? Do you pay your bills the day they're due or even afterwards? Do you lose track of all those due dates? Or perhaps you've been wanting to start an emergency fund, but every time you plan to open the account, an emergency derails your savings plan.

The mere thought of discussing money makes some stress and break out in a cold sweat. Classic avoidance has been the modus operandi for others. Yet there are those who say they need to change but do not take the necessary steps to change. None of these will give you the needful results of a healthy financial future.

If you're not transparent about your current financial status, the probability of you falling into unfortunate (and credit-damaging) habits is highly likely.

ASK ME HOW I KNOW! I was intimately acquainted with the struggle. I lived from paycheck to paycheck, hoping and praying no emergencies popped up that would send me into a tailspin. I wholeheartedly believed I was doing ok when I was able to pay my bills. But the wind was knocked out of me when I was no longer working, and I had to live off my savings.

I quickly realized I was not adequately prepared for the storm. I was too busy living for the moment instead of preparing for the future.

Through many tears, lost battles, repeated lessons and forced reality check, I saw that the real enemy was M-E! I was fighting against my own forward progress. I blamed others for my mess because it couldn't *possibly* be me. Nah, not the kid! It just couldn't be the lack of balanced accounts, lack of emergency funds or the delinquent payments that got me to where I was. It wasn't the frivolous spending, emotional purchases, and impulse buys. It wasn't the expensive trips, the overstocked closets and the constantly wasted food from the fridge. It was clearly not the frequent visits to restaurants. Clearly, I was not the issue.

I had to get real with myself. The sum of where I was financially (and in life overall) was from the choices I had made. Some situations may have been beyond my control, but my responses to them had everything to do with me and my decisioning. Facing my finances was not easy but I had to take ownership of my behavior. If I wanted different results, I had to not only change my behavior but start with changing my mindset. Eventually I shifted from working for money to making money work for me.

This was not an overnight change. There was a progression of steps I took to redeem my time and money. One way I jumpstarted my journey to Charity 2.0 was through a spending fast. At the beginning of each year, some people make goals and resolutions of doing and being better. We make lofty plans of loss and gain… losing that fluffy status (because the pandemic did a number on us!) and gaining that fit and fine body. Letting go of that dead end, energy draining job and starting that business. Letting go of negative thinking AND people and gaining peace. For many, it will be a time to give up a personal vice – numerous people opt out of chocolate or alcohol. It may come in the form of a fast from social networks and even the cell phone. Why not take it a step further and do a fast from spending to help gain perspective and control.

I put a pause on my spending, except for paying bills and only getting life-essential things (groceries, gas, etc.). So that meant putting a moratorium on shopping for clothes, shoes, hair, makeup, dining out, even helping people out of a bind. It was time to help myself. Just as the flight instructions tell you to put the mask on yourself before trying to assist others, it was time that I focus on helping me out of my space. No amount of crying was going to change me or my situation. Prayer alone was not going to change me. YUP. I SAID WHAT I SAID. I had to stop expecting God to do what He's enabled and empowered me to do. I had no maintenance plan in place had I received a miracle. I had to stop hiding behind prayer and put the work in. I decided I had been easy on myself long enough and it was past time for tough love and a new type of self-care. I was no longer going to hitch a ride on the self-love and self-care bandwagon to "protect my peace" when I was the very one posing a threat to my peace, protection, provision, and prosperity. Yes, I knew and understood that I had to give myself some grace but that did not mean give myself an escape from truth and discipline.

I quickly learned the difference between a want and a need. After reviewing my spending habits, more than 60% of what I was spending was on wants. I did not need more clothes. I DEFINITELY did not need more shoes. I did not need cable. I did not NEED a big wedding (that one hurt the most).

This deep detox helped to bring up and out what was ailing my finances. Think about it. During a fast, not only is weight lost, but each system has a chance to detox, rest, and regroup. The body is ridding itself of toxins and things that weigh it down and cause sluggish function. Additionally, one of my favorite benefits from a fast is mental clarity. The brain's function increases because it's not at war for energy to process extra weight and material from constant consumption.

While on the spending fast, I not only put the brakes on spending, but I also focused on the way I viewed money, developed short, mid, and long-term goals, increased my financial literacy, and got an accountability partner to hold me to my goals. I challenged myself to become more resourceful…from curating new meals from leftovers, date nights in and movies in the backyard to arts and crafts with the kids in the basement. I discovered a joy and peace that money could not buy. A bonus from the spending fast was that it brought my husband, children, and I closer and even motivated our family and friends to participate. We began to help each other, share tips and suggestions, and encourage each other to stick to the plan. Our mindset shifted from one of sacrifice and misery (because let's face it, spending is fun!), to having fun with being creative. We realized we could save without feeling unhappy. We found fun, free activities in our communities. We rediscovered the vast selection of books and movies at the local library. It also cost us nothing to reengage in hobbies like writing, reading, listening to music, playing games at home, and cooking our meals. We were so motivated and excited that we even started calling ourselves the Never Broke Nation! Day by day, we were changing for the better, financially, mentally, and physically. Our Never Broke Nation thrived on truth, trust, and transparency to help and hold each other accountable.

Although the fast was good, I didn't just stop there; what's the point of fasting and detoxing if I returned to the same behavior that had me in a financial stupor. I turned that moment into a fiscal movement. From budgeting and opening businesses to getting a financial planner, I now took my financial future very seriously. Truthfully, I am still a work in progress. I've not fully arrived but I am striving to stay on the path that secures my future.

Your story may be like mine... financial battles, disorganized with paying bills, inconsistent with saving, and struggling to build a financial future. No matter what your current position is, there's good news. You can and will whip your finances into shape with discipline, organization, and patience. Become so committed to managing your finances that every dollar has a mission. Don't wait until the new year....START NOW, WHEREVER YOU ARE! Make minor changes to have a major impact not just in the immediate future but also for generations to come. It all starts with a mindset to adopt and adapt to change. Learn from your past, then pivot. Do not lament. LEARN!

So, my recommendation to you is this: get informed and apply pressure! You're already searching for a solution, which brought you here. You're off to a great start but don't stop here. Put into practice the tips, utilize the tools and leverage the trainings to position you to gain financial freedom.

Come along with me on this journey to REFLECT, REDIRECT AND RECONCILE your finances. Buckle up buttercup…you are on your way to becoming a savvier saver, investor, and spender.

PHASE 1

REFLECT

Reflect · /rĭ-flĕkt'/[1]

verb
to think seriously; to think, meditate, or ponder

During this time of reflection, you will be doing a checkup from the neck up by assessing where you are and how you got there.

Fasting and detoxing is a shock to your system. It's dramatic, it's drastic, it's intense but necessary. The hardest time of the spending fast is the first 5-7 days, when you will be doing a lot of spending reviews and taking an introspective look at the whys of your spending. Just as a physical fast and detox will have you feeling like you're going through withdrawal symptoms, so too will you experience the 'shakes' as you begin to thoroughly review your finances and tell yourself NO to buying that pair of shoes! Your mind and wallet are saying "I DON'T LIKE THIS DENIAL. SPENDING FEELS GOOD. IT GIVES SATISFACTION (HIGH). I see something, I want it, I get it, EVEN IF I DON'T NEED IT." I'll tell on myself….I can't begin to tell you the number of unworn pairs of shoes, the amount of clothes in the closet still with tags, exercise equipment that now doubles as storage space and not to mention the inordinate collection of unreturned Redbox DVDs.

Let the non-judgmental journey to better understand your money and you begin.

REMEMBER, THIS IS A JOURNEY OF TRUTH, TRUST, AND TRANSPARENCY.

DAY 1

Looking Back to Move Forward

"You live life looking forward, you understand life looking backward."

~ Soren Kierkegaard

To map a clear path for your financial future, you will need to understand where you are and how you got there. The first step is realizing how much you spend and then labeling that spend as a need or want. You can do this by gathering your credit card and bank statements from the last six months. This period will give you a holistic view of your spending, as some months may have had more spend than others (based on holidays, birthdays, anniversaries, back to school, etc.). Highlight your needs in one color and your wants in another. You might be surprised at how much you are spending on your wants as opposed to your needs.

Second, take an honest assessment of what's really a need versus a want. The deciding factor often depends on how and why you use that expense. To that, there is a chasmic gap in how we identify what is a need versus what really is a need. For example, cable might seem like a need, but it is most definitely a want. Home internet may be a need for you if you work from home. However, if you only use your home internet for entertainment, such as browsing social media or playing video games, it is a want. Going to the salon/barber, getting manicures and pedicures may be a part of your self-care regimen. I totally get it. Yes, self-care is necessary for life balance but going to the salon to get your hair done is

19

not a need. It's a want. Even your cell phone could be a want. I understand that cell phones are essential to staying accessible to family and work so, in many cases, a cell phone is a need as it is a means of communication. However, you can accomplish that with a $20 flip phone. If you choose instead to spend hundreds of dollars on a new smartphone, that extra expense is suddenly a want. Also, it could be possible that you are grossly overpaying for an unlimited plan with special features that you rarely, or even worse, don't use.

With these examples in mind, revisit your bank and credit card statements, and rethink what is really a need versus a want. Here's a way to break down those primary needs:

1. **Housing:** Mortgage and rent are needs.
2. **Utilities:** Gas, water, heat, and electricity are needs.
3. **Food:** Food is undoubtedly a need, but it can also be a want in many ways.
4. **Transportation:** Primarily, this is a need.
5. **Savings:** This is a need.

TIP

- Remember, needs include ***basics*** like food, shelter, and clothing. Wants, on the other hand, are material items you can live without, but desire to own. You need food to avoid hunger, a roof over your head and clothing, but those needs can quickly morph into wants when they become a banquet, ten room estate and luxury wardrobe.

DAY 2

YOUR MONEY MINDSET

"The greatest discovery of all time is that a person can change his
future
by merely changing his attitude."
~Oprah Winfrey

Secure the bag! Collect the coins! Get that check! Hustle hard! Be on your grind! Bring home the bacon!

Getting and having money is not a terrible thing. It's not inherently evil and the reality is we all need it, yet the paper chase can be unrelenting and flat-out tiring! From 16ish to retirement (and even beyond), one of the most predominate thoughts is accumulating money. It's on everybody's mind, but no one is supposed to talk about it. It's all around us from Black Wall Street to Manhattan to the Champs Elysée. Even our music complains about and celebrates it. From songs crying about the troubles with having a lot of money (*Mo Money Mo Problems, Old Money, Gold Digger*), the beauty of having too much of it (*Super Rich Kids, Tom Ford, Luxurious*), or the reality that most are chasing paper at the end of the day (*C.R.E.A.M., Money (That's What I Want)*), we are inundated and forced to think about money.

So, how do you think about money? What's the first thing that comes to your mind? Do you get excited with the limitless possibilities of making it? Do you think of ways to grow it? Do you get stressed out thinking about how much you have for retirement? Do you get pissed because all you do is work to pay bills? Do you get sad by how little you have? For many people, money is a dictator. The course of your day and your level of peace and happiness depends on how much money you have.

It's no secret that the wealthy have a unique way of thinking about money than the average person does. Money is something they have plenty of, have little to no problem acquiring it, and have no fear of spending it. From the outside looking in, it's easy to say that their wealth mindset is an offshoot of their accumulated money.

Before getting too presumptuous, consider their life before becoming wealthy. While some of the super-rich were born into an inheritance, many self-made millionaires had to acquire their wealth on their own, having the battle scars to prove it. Their rags-to-riches testimonies tell of the trials, toils, and triumphs in their journey to financial independence. Their mindset and resolve to succeed was unrelenting.

Whether self-made or inherited, what is the difference between where you are and where the wealthy are? THE MINDSET! The first major disparity in how the wealthy vs the working class (and I use that term very loosely) think is how they define money. For many, money is regarded as an end result in exchange for the time and service provided (more than likely at a job of some sort). Something we earn for working. Something we lose when it's spent. This earned money is what is used to pay bills as well as create and sustain lifestyles, but seldom does the average person think of money as an actual tool. For the wealthy, they view money as a tool to be used to acquire and do more of what they really want. Crowd funders, major investors, venture capitalists and the likes understand this concept. Their success is largely contingent on their ability to view and use money as a tool for investments.

To better explain this concept, let's imagine you've been given $1 million after taxes, and you need to buy a car[2]. Most people would buy the car, cash on sight. After all, you have a million dollars at your disposal and the price of a $30,000 car does not have a major impact on your money. The wealthy would decide to finance this new car, which will have an average monthly payment of $800. The wealthy minded person may place the million dollars in a savings account that yields a 1% return, then use the $833 per month of accumulated interest to pay for the car. Instead of spending money on the car and taking away from that extra million, the wealthy get to keep their million dollars and get the car too.

From this example, you can begin to see the difference in how money is viewed and thus apportioned. When you start to view money as a tool, that mindset allows you to grow your wealth and do more of what you want in life. If you do not have a mindset to master money and use it as a tool, you could make mistakes that have a negative impact over time. Just look at lottery winners and those in sports and entertainment. Because many of them come into a windfall without a proper money mindset or a plan to generate and grow wealth, they end up in a worse position than prior to getting the big bucks. Statistics show that 70% of lottery winners end up broke or declaring bankruptcy within seven years[3]. Many get caught up in the euphoria of the perceived power they now possess. The spending spigot gets turned on and it never gets turned off. Most quit their job without a plan in place so money is steadily going out, but nothing is coming in.

If you are one day blessed to experience a windfall from lottery, a settlement, an endowment, insurance, or any other means, ensure you have the proper attitude about money as well as the proper team in place to help you manage it, at minimum a financial planner.

Another mindset shift needs to focus on how wealth is accumulated. The average person relies heavily on their job to pay debt, save, and fund their retirement. They depend on this one source to finance the entire lot of their current and future life. The wealthy function much differently. First, they don't see their jobs, careers, work as their source; they see it as a resource. Secondly, the wealthy will have multiple resources to prosper in their present and finance their future. This is called diversification, or what I term *insulated wealth* ™. They may have real estate, own businesses, invest in the stock market and so much more. You can even look at entertainment. Gone are the days of actors building their legacy with just movies. They are not only acting in movies, but they are also creating podcasts, doing television commercials, providing voiceovers for varied brands, starting their own companies, have speaking engagements, and make guest appearances. These are all multiple resources that feed into their diversified portfolio.

You may not be at that point of having such a vast portfolio but begin to think about how you can shift your mindset away from putting all your eggs in one basket by depending on one resource to diversifying your resources. We will talk more about this later (Multiple Streams of Income).

TIP

- Focus more on the future. Many people get stuck focusing on paying off bills and debt. It's such a powerful theme in their lives that all their attention, with regards to money accumulation, is centered around paying bills and reducing their debt. While it's great to pay your bills on time and reduce your debt, you can't let it distract you from creating wealth.

DAY 3

EMOTIONAL SPENDING

"Create a life that feels good on the inside, not one that just looks good on the outside."

~Author unknown

One summer day when I was 12 years old, I had begun to experience severe pain in my lower right side. Not sure what was happening, my parents gave me a pain reliever and antacid to alleviate the pain. Well, that didn't work. The pain became progressively worse and eventually became unbearable. I was unable to stand and could not control any of my bodily functions. Needless to say, I was rushed to the hospital and was diagnosed as having acute appendicitis with septic shock (commonly known as toxic shock). This was quite a dangerous situation, in that life-threatening toxins were being released throughout my body, causing it to go into shock, so the staff quickly began to push fluids and antibiotics through my body to flush out the toxins. The pain and loss of function were the needful indicators to communicate something was not working properly in my body.

I know your beautiful brilliance is wondering what this has to do with finances. In short, EVERYTHING. This discomfort and pain that you are feeling in your finances is working in overdrive to convey that something is misaligned with your mind, mood, and money. The more you try to alleviate the discomfort and dissonance with a purchase, the worse the pain becomes. Eventually, it can bring you to a complete halt. This is what I've coined as *toxic spending syndrome™* or more commonly known as emotional spending.

Just as toxic shock sets up poison throughout the body, threatening life itself, so too can toxic spending syndrome affect every area of your life. It can threaten the health of your mind, body, soul, and spirit and can cause imbalance in life, marriage, and relationships. Your mind and your money are at civil war within you, and it is wreaking havoc on your fiscal focus.

I had to face the harsh reality that I suffered from toxic spending syndrome. In troubled times, I spent. In good times, I spent. When I began to do an autopsy on my past spending, I realized that much of my spending was done during times where I was facing challenges in life. I overcompensated for feelings of inadequacy, thoughts of being less than and to combat depression. Whenever I was overlooked, undervalued, underappreciated, misunderstood or just flat out unhappy, I shopped (and ate, to be perfectly honest) to attempt to replace those feelings. I shopped when I felt my clothes were not good enough for the occasion or person/people I was going out with during that time.

The toxicity didn't stop there. Needless spending was also my way of celebrating me. I hid behind the guise of self-care and 'loving on me.' I psyched my mind to believe, 'oh I deserve this; I've earned this retail therapy for all my hard work.' I spent (and ate) when I accomplished a personal goal or had a major win with a project.

Emotional Spending

It's one thing to realize you're with toxic people, it's a sad, sobering gut punch to realize that you are toxic to yourself. I had to recognize I was my worst enemy. I was the one blocking my blessings. My spending was the weapon formed against my finances.

After my financial awakening, I began to put the work in, first by doing the previously mentioned 6-month spending review and then by noting how I felt at the time of current purchases. I stopped letting myself off easy, giving myself a 'get out of jail free card.' I had to stop allowing a bruised ego to dictate what I would do financially (and socially and spiritually and emotionally for that matter). I had to admit that spending may solve a temporary pain, but it did not address the root of why I was feeling and spending that way.

So determined to break the cycle, I ripped the bandage off and addressed the root of the issues. So not being promoted was a trigger of unaddressed low self-worth. Being overlooked was a trigger of unaddressed feelings of inadequacy. I was so drowning in emotional imbalance that even something as slight as being cut off mid-sentence triggered feelings of being devalued. Being talked about triggered feelings of disrespect. Feeling unheard…. trigger. Feeling judged…. trigger. Feeling out of control…. trigger. Yes, facing those facts hurt but not changing was killing me financially and emotionally!

I knew it was past time that I faced the issues directly and put the work in to change my narrative. I had to ask myself, "what does it take to make me happy?" After I got past the superficial things like money, dream houses, cars and trips, the core of what makes me happy is love, peace, family, and having balance. I also realized that I had been sacrificing my happiness for the comfort of others. I had left the core of who I was and was trying to dress up the variant of me with clothes and a career. Sure, I experienced happy moments, but I was not authentically happy because I was not at peace and happy with myself internally and externally.

I had allowed an imposter syndrome to creep in and consume my life; even though I projected an air of confidence and had success in my professional and personal life, I constantly doubted my abilities, talents, education and accomplishments and assigned my value based on what I had and what others felt I was worth; their opinions had become my reality. I realized that most of what I did was for the acceptance, approval, and validation of others. This had a major impact on how I spent money; I had to ensure I projected an image of confidence, beauty, and sexiness.

Once I got to the root cause of perfectionism and the insatiable desire to overachieve covering for the real need to be accepted, I had to retrain my brain. I literally looked myself in the mirror and said "CHARITY, YOU ARE ENOUGH, JUST AS YOU ARE, WITHOUT ANY FILTER, FILLER, OR FAÇADE. You are worthy of happiness. You are deserving of genuine love." I had to relearn how to accept and appreciate who God had created me to be. I embraced my God-given destiny and decided I would no long dishonor or disgrace my purpose by not showing up as a fully self-accepted me.

So now I am asking you…. Are there any triggers that are linked to unresolved issues in your life? Are you stimulating the economy because of a refusal to take ownership of your emotional toil? What does happiness and peace look like for you? Here's a clue…. money will not make you happy. It may make you comfortable, but it cannot bring true happiness. Even if you have millions, you're a poor person with millions because you lack health and happiness in your spirit and soul. It's not the money, it's a mindset. Until you fill that space, you will be in lack. You've been searching all over the world looking for answers, looking through religions, searching horoscopes, turning to shopping and eating yet you remain unfulfilled.

God is the answer. When you ask Him to come into your life, things will change. It may not change overnight. It may still hurt. Yet because you have now invited God to be in the equation, the outcome will be different. He's there to help you, lead and guide you. It's as simple as saying God I need you. Jesus, save me. I can no longer do this on my own. Help me. I can't change on my own. I don't have the answers I'm searching for. I'm drained and tapped out mentally, emotionally, socially, and financially. I've tried religion but now I need a relationship.

When you allow God to heal you from the inside out…. destroying the root of your issues, the fruit that you previously displayed will begin to change. Having the God-factor in your life can and will help you address emotions that effect your spending, such as guilt (because it's just too hard to say no to those sweet babies selling Girl Scout Cookies), jealousy (you just have to keep up with the Joneses), sadness (a bad week deserves retail therapy), fear (let me hurry up and take out a second mortgage on my home before this housing bubble pops) and anger (am I the only one who has made purchases in anger a time or ten to get back at their spouse? No, just me? Ok.), to name a few.

Now that you are armed with the knowledge of emotions and moods having a way of directing your spending behavior, you can begin to create a defensive plan to counterattack this behavior. First, identify your triggers, then note how you feel when you make a purchase. Identify what drives you to spend. Are you sad, did you just have a rough day at work, did you have a disagreement with your mate, is it the anniversary of a loved one's death, did you just get some unwelcomed news, are you celebrating an accomplishment? Keep a log of your spending and the activities and emotions surrounding that purchase, including the time of day (you may tend to spend at night when you feel alone). Here are some additional tips to help you keep focused on your financial health.

TIP

- Enforce the 24 to 48-hour rule. While shopping for things you want, leave them in your online shopping cart for 24 to 48 hours. This is your cool down period to avoid making impulse buys.

DAY 4

DECLUTTER AND PURGE

"Clutter is nothing more than postponed decisions."
~Barbara Hempill

We reside in a world where a materialistic culture screams that the more things you have, the happier you will be. The opposite is true. The more you consume, the greater likelihood you will create a cluttered environment, which lends itself to producing stagnant energy and increased anxiety from feelings of being overwhelmed.

Clutter is defined by Dictionary.com as a state or condition of confusion, to fill with things in a disorderly manner. From clean laundry that remains unfolded and put away in a cluttered closet and dirty dishes in the sink to an increasing number of 'junk drawers' and a chaotic mess of a garage, this resounding theme of household pandemonium can creep up and overtake your life if left unchecked. It's sometimes challenging to identify your precious items as clutter so here are a few questions to help you face the music:

- Does it have a place to land or live?
- Does it no longer serve a purpose to you?
- Is it broken or does it need repair?
- Is it messy?
- Is it organized chaos?

- Has it become challenging to manage?

I get it…parting is such sweet sorrow, yet so many people are living in physical (and emotional) clutter which can lead to unhappiness, stress and even depression[4]; these emotions have the potential to lead to emotional spending as a triggering coping mechanism.

Previously I mentioned emotional spending and the effects it has on finances. This can lead to overspending and a closet full of 'stuff' that you are not using or wearing. I cannot begin to tell you how many articles of clothes, purses, hats, and shoes that still have tags on them in my closet, along with gym equipment that has collected dust.

The average woman in the U.S. have approximately $2,500 worth of items in their closets (unless you're a part of the nearly 10% of women whose closet is worth over $10,000).[5] Additionally, 50% of women don't wear 25% of their wardrobe, which is about $625 worth of clothes wasted, not to mention over 5,000 wasted hours[6] in our lifetime looking for lost items in our closet. The average person spends 2.5 days each year looking for lost items, collectively costing U.S. households $2.7 billion annually in replacement costs.[7] You may be thinking, "nah I KNOW I don't waste that much time, after all, it doesn't take me that long to find my stuff." Well, you would be surprised. Let the numbers speak for themselves. The average time you spend looking for something is between 1 and 15 minutes, which doesn't seem too bad. But if this is every day, that's 420 hours a month, 2,520 hours in 6 months and 5,040 hours in a year, spent looking for things in a cluttered environment. This is a sobering reality of time being money. What could you accomplish with 5,000 hours? That's 29.8 weeks. That's 208 days.

- The average time to write the first draft to a book for most authors is 180 days (~26 weeks)
- The average time to start an at-home business is 45 days (6 weeks)
- The average time to get a real estate license is 14-72 days (2-6 weeks)
- The average time to train for a marathon is 112-140 days (16 to 20 weeks)
- The average time to complete a continuing education course such as PMP is

Before you buy another article of clothing, another pair of shoes, another kitchen gadget, another piece of exercise equipment, take inventory of what you already have. Start with one of your spaces. For this example, we will start with your closet. Empty out the entire contents of your closet. Drastic, yest but it will pay off in the end. Neatly lay them all out on your bed, floor, or wherever you can find adequate space.

Create a pile for each of the following categories: sell, keep, donate, and discard. Try on each item to ensure fit and function then determine which of the four piles to which they'll go.

Sell

If your items are still in excellent condition but don't fit you anymore, whether in size or style, then consider selling your clothes in a consignment shop or via online stores such as TheRealReal, Poshmark, Tradesy, Luxury Garage Sale, or ThredUP.

Keep

The "keep" pile is comprised of items you can fit, love and will repeatedly wear.

Donate

Clothes that are still decent but not in top condition to consign can go in this donate pile. Giving it away to a non-profit organization will provide a tax-deduction for you!

Discard

Unless you are a creative person and/or tailor, clothes that are completely worn out and falling apart need to be discarded. If you're upcycling them, give yourself two weeks to complete the project, otherwise it's trash.

After you finish with your closet, head to the next space that needs decluttering and apply the same process.

TIP

- When returning the clothes to the closet for the 'keep' pile, turn your hangers in the opposite direction of how you would normally place them. If after six months, they are in the same position, that's your indicator that you have not touched that piece of clothing in six months, so it's time to let it go. Same with your shoes and purses. Exceptions are given to formal wear and swimwear. Other than that, everything in your closet is fair game. Don't give yourself the excuse of seasonal wear. A sundress can be worn in multiple seasons. Put a blazer, belt, and pair of boots with that sundress and voila, you have a repurposed outfit for a different season.

DAY 5

MARRIAGE AND MONEY

"Each partner must keep in mind that most relationships aren't destroyed by one dramatic act, but by a series of small, inconsequential acts that chip away at your foundation of love and trust."

~Mindy Crary

Talking about money isn't exactly romantic pillow talk but it is essential, as the number one cause for divorce is money (followed by infidelity and lack of healthy and effective communication). To thrive in your partnership, regular, transparent money management conversations are crucial. This goes beyond discussing bills and savings. Initially, this was a bit challenging for me. As a single woman, I was so accustomed to doing my own thing without the need to 'check in' with anyone. Sure, while dating, during our engagement and in premarital counseling (I wholeheartedly recommend this), we discussed finances, credit usage, debt and who would be responsible for household management.

The more Gary and I discussed finances, the more I felt uncomfortable having the type of wedding I was planning to have (let's face it ladies, it's our wedding). Although I was savvy about getting a gorgeous custom dress for $100 and was able to buy the decorations wholesale, I still did not have a peace about how we were entering our marriage financially. As much as it hurt me not to have the wedding of my dreams, I knew in my heart that scaling back and using the money to pay down debt was the

38

best decision. I had to get away from the fairytale fantasy as well as societal dictates of what a wedding should be and do what was best for our finances. The wedding was for one day, but we must live after that. Am I going to be so focused on the one day that I negate the comforts of living after that day is done?

Even after the 'I DOs' were said and rings were exchanged, it was hard for me to jump on the merged money mindset bandwagon. I agreed with it in principle, but it took some years for me to get adjusted. It was not until Gary and I developed a mission statement for our marriage and listed out our financial goals that I really let go of the 'me-my-mines' mindset and adapted to the 'ours' reality. In addition to our mission and goal statement, we set a spending cap. We were able to spend up to $50 without informing one another. Anything over that amount required a conversation. With me being Loophole Linda, I found ways around this agreement by breaking up my purchases into multiple transactions. I tell you….if Amazon had a loyalty program that provided frequent flyer miles based on spend, I could have earned a trip to Tahiti! Just saying!

I knew I had to reel in my spending when I left my job; things got REAL for me. The truth of my out-of-control lifestyle came to a head when I was staring down the barrel of unemployment. I took a hard look at my behavior and accepted full responsibility for where I was financially. Because of a lack of discipline, our savings were nowhere near what they could have been; I had gotten comfortable with being comfortable instead of being more aggressive with our financial future. "After all, the kids have a savings account, we're making deposits into our savings, and nothing's behind in our household" was the justification in my head, yet I was making minimum payments and the credit cards which once had a zero balance now had crept up again. I was suffering from financial infidelity, which can have a similar impact on a marriage as physical and emotional infidelity[8].

"Financial infidelity is the secretive act of spending money, hiding your purchases, having secret credit accounts and credit cards, holding secret 'mad money' accounts or stashes, borrowing money without informing your spouse (even if borrowed from family or friend), or incurring debt without informing your spouse. Financial infidelity in a relationship may also include any financial decision(s) made by a partner that may affect, burden, strain or set back the financial planning of the relationship[9]." No matter the type of financial infidelity, it all points back to a breach of truth, trust, and transparency.

I felt because I wasn't hiding my big purchases and he had access to my accounts and passwords, I was ok, but I had to be honest with myself and take ownership of my financially infidel ways. I sincerely apologized but I had to give more than just lip service; I had to make a 180° turn from my behavior and mindset. Since quitting my job with no job immediately lined up, I had time to focus on precisely that... where we were financially and what my contribution was to it. Through many candid conversations and acknowledgement of emotional turmoil, I made a serious commitment to myself and Gary to be honest about how I'm feeling, list what steps and tools we needed to take to better position us for financial success and be consistent to our goals. Two things that I implemented immediately were my foregoing my monthly massages and my bi-weekly manicure/pedicures. Now, Gary and I have our own massage table and we give each other massages. We also do each other's pedicures biweekly. Not only are we saving money, but we are creating greater intimacy in our relationship.

We have conversations on a weekly basis on our spending and savings as well as investments and overall goals conversations twice a month. We are intentional on remaining on the same page and moving together. We are also now dreaming together. I love doing this with Gary. If we had millions at our disposal, how would we spend it? Who would we help? What organizations would we contribute to, and how would we invest in ourselves, businesses, and community? It costs us nothing to dream, so why not dream big!

As Gary and I talked through our issues and put a working plan in place, so too do I recommend you have those money talks. Discuss your financial goals, review your mission statement, talk about your dreams. This will help to see if your activities are aligning and moving you towards or away from your goals.

If talking about money is difficult for you and your spouse, go to a neutrally peaceful place you both enjoy outside of the home and ask these questions[10] (remember to respectfully allow them to answer and be truthful with your own responses to the questions):

- What is your most painful money memory?
- What is your most joyful money memory?

- How did these experiences shape your relationship with money?
- What three things did your parents or family teach you about money?
- Which lessons have you applied to your financial life?
- Growing up, did you see your family as rich, poor, or middle class?
- What were your family's values about money?
- What is your greatest financial fear?
- What are you willing to do differently when it comes to money?

TIP

- When having your money talks, leave society's dictates of how your household should run out of your discussions and decisioning. Don't let other people's relationship rules and blueprint be your standard. ***DO WHAT WORKS BEST FOR YOUR HOUSEHOLD***.

DAY 6

WHAT IS YOUR WHY

"If you can't figure out your purpose, figure out your passion; that passion will lead you into your purpose."
~Thomas Dexter Jakes

It wouldn't be a stretch to say that no one wants to live a life forever owing and being in debt. It is quite common to want more, be more, do more in life. BUT WHY? Why do you want more money? Why do you want to be out of debt? Discovering your why is mission critical to help find your focus and target your energy.

Why are you saving money?
Why are you seeking financial independence?
Why are you making financial sacrifices?
What is your motivation and motivator?
What are your goals?
What is the end game?
What is the fuel that's driving your passion to be debt free?

Having an emotionally driven 'why' keeps you connected to your corresponding actions. Whether you desire to pay off student loans, build an emergency reserve, pay off your mortgage, save for your child(ren)'s college fund, save for your wedding, or travel to your dream destination and ball out while there, having your 'why' at the forefront of your mind and in eye's view (can you say vision board) helps you to remain resolute when times get challenging and when it's time to decide that the $400 a

43

month you spend in eating out can be smartly used to pay your mortgage off early and simultaneously invest in stocks and IRAs.

To build a strong 'why,' consider what's most valuable to you and your family, what gives you purpose and meaning. The goal is to **find a mission for your money**. It could be as intimate as being financially free to care for your aging parents, be a stay-at-home mom or as grand as resolve the water shortage in East Sudan and help end food deserts in urban areas. Whatever it is, your WHY must be BIGGER THAN YOU. When your mission transcends making money, it becomes a powerful driver. So, when you build a strong 'why,' you increase your likelihood to succeed.

With your 'why' comes the responsibility to educate yourself, open your mind, and expand beyond your comfort zone. You can't just sit back and depend on others to run your financial show. As smart as it is to have a financial advisor, they aren't necessarily motivated by your 'why.' And let me help you.... Don't expect everyone to understand or agree with your 'why.' Become settled and find affirmation within yourself on your motivation and motivators. Only YOU will find power in that.

My primary 'why' is to set a better tone and future for my children and their children. Leaving a secure legacy of financial literacy and inheritance is the fuel that drives me to keep sacrificing. Knowing that my children's children's children will be financially secure for life keeps me pushing past immediate gratification. I am determined to leave the next generation in a better position to go further, do more, and be better than us.

Another 'why' for my intense drive to succeed financially is to have enough savings, investments, and cash on hand to afford the kind of life my husband and I desire for ourselves and our families. We are steadily moving towards growing our savings to the point that we are financially enabled to retire at-will or pursue the career we want without being driven by earning a set salary each year. My 'why' for financial freedom means our money is working for us versus us spending most of our time relentlessly grinding and hustling for money. When Gary and I started on our journey to debt and financial freedom, we were so thrilled when we saw our debt decreasing. The more we paid off, the more excited AND desperate we became to get out of debt. That desperation and excitement were constant motivators.

An additional 'why' is because I have a fervent desire to help people end the negative financial cycles they've experienced and chart a new path to financial freedom. I am motivated to leverage my learnings from my former lack of knowledge, bad learned behavior, poor decisioning and plain ol' laziness. You don't have to make the mistakes I've made; your journey does not have to be hard, long, or convoluted. Educating, empowering, equipping, and motivating the masses is what drives my passion to help you push past any limitations you or others have set.

TIP

- Write down your 'whys.' These will become the basis for your goals. Having a rock-solid WHY is the foundation of success. Accumulating money for the sake of not being broke is a valid why, albeit very surface. Without a strong 'why' attached to it, your money won't accomplish *much* for you.

DAY 7

PREPARING FOR INCREASE

"Proper preparation prevents poor performance and procrastination."
~James Baker

If someone comes to you and says 'I want to pay off all your debt and pay your household expenses, inclusive of property taxes and all forms of insurance, for five years, would you have that figure readily available? Is your financial house clean, decluttered, and ready to receive more? If you cannot truthfully answer yes to both, you've got work to do to prepare for an increase.

Do you know how much it takes, down to the penny, to become debt free? Do you know what your monthly household expenditures are? Do you know what's going out and coming in financially? Do you have an emergency fund established? Do you have health insurance and life insurance? Do you have a living will? How much are you allocating towards savings, retirement, investing? Are you in a place to manage a windfall, whether it's from lottery, a settlement, or an insurance benefit? Are you managing being a hundredaire and thousandaire, while you're praying and playing (Vegas is consistently packed) to be a millionaire?

We're a "manifest it" society. I wholeheartedly believe in the power of positive thinking, and to that I add actions and consistency to help manifest my desire for increase. Some of you may not be mentally prepared to oversee more. You could be in the same place, if not, in a

47

worse place financially if you received more. Put the work in to position yourself to be good stewards of what you have while preparing to receive more.

TIP

- Start with your credit report to begin gathering your debt footprint. Then add in those items that may not show up on the report, such as medical bills being paid.

PHASE 2
REDIRECT

Redirect · /rē′dĭ-rĕkt′/[11]

verb
To cause to move in a different direction or go to a different destination:

During your spending fast, you will spend the bulk of your time in this phase. In Redirect, you will learn and leverage tools to change the trajectory of your financial path. The goal is to help reposition you while you heal from the inside out. Many pray and play to become millionaires but struggle being thousandaires.

Let's fully immerse and embrace your new normal of budgeting and balancing finances and life.

DAY 8

BABY STEPS

"The secret of getting ahead is getting started. The secret of getting started is breaking complex, overwhelming tasks into small manageable tasks, and then starting on the first one."

~Mark Twain

Now that you are on your journey to you 2.0, give yourself the grace and space to run your race at your pace. I know you want to be at your financial destination of being debt free right now, but you must pace yourself for the long haul. As a marathoner, I know the value of the phrase, 'it's a marathon and not a sprint.' Even if your start is small and feels meager, don't despise it. The baby steps are the building blocks on which you are building a strong legacy.

Think about a baby. When they are learning to walk, they are not only taking small steps, but there's also a continuum in their progression. These sweet babies have an excitement and determination to walk. Although they fall many times, they don't let that discourage them to the point of stopping and never trying again. No, they get back up, sometimes with tears running down those precious cheeks and continue to try. Eventually they get it. Eventually the coordination comes. With continued practice throughout the day, their motor skills increase, they get accustomed to those new legs. Soon, they set their sights on the next level, running.

Our baby girl Hannah was walking at 10 months. It was the most awkward, uncoordinated and, at times, painful thing to watch. Yet her joy and enthusiasm in "getting it" far outweighed the pain of the moment. She didn't make a permanent decision to not walk based on the temporary inconvenience of falling and making uncoordinated steps.

Take the cues from a child learning to walk. Become child-like with your finances. You may have to take baby steps. They may start off small, uncoordinated, jarring, and off balance, but DO NOT STOP. Don't quit when you feel pain. Don't quit if you fall. Don't quit if you miss the mark. Don't quit if you feel you're alone on this journey. Don't quit if your back is against the wall and you must decide on necessity vs. nonessential.

So what you messed up. This is a process. You are developing. You don't come into this with all the wisdom, all the understanding, in full maturity regarding saving and budgeting. Just as a person does not develop muscles after a week of working out at the gym, so too will you not be a full financial guru after a week, even a year of budgeting, saving, investing, and learning. It takes time. Give yourself grace to grow! Allow yourself the room to learn and develop. You are discovering things about yourself....your spending habits, your emotional triggers, your mindset on money, your money's purpose, and mission. Allow the process to give what it needs to give.

Should you mess up, 'fess up and don't prolong the process by saying 'I'll start again next month.' NO KEEP GOING RIGHT NOW. Change

52

is sometimes hard and does not feel good. But guess what…. STAYING THE SAME IS JUST AS, IF NOT, MORE PAINFUL! It will hurt if you do not change AND it will hurt as you change.

Remaining unchanged can be a terminal detriment to you but change is a temporary pain that has the potential to become a glorious generational game-changer in the end. SO, PICK YOUR PAIN. Will it be permanence from remaining the same or will you commit to change? I set before you life and death, blessings and curses. Choose ye this day. I'll give you a hint…. CHOOSE LIFE! Choose a financial life that will bring healing, health, and happiness to not only yourself but those around you.

TIP

- Keep a diary of your goals and the steps you are taking. One of the most rewarding feelings is being able to check off a goal you've accomplished.

DAY 9

Giving Life to Leftovers and Lists

"Show your creative side by remixing your meal. Most call it leftovers but I choose to call it curating a new culinary experience."

~C. Ann Morris

'Ugh. There's nothing in here to cook.' How many of you have said that as you blankly stared in your fridge? Before going grocery shopping again, use what you already have in your fridge and freezer first. Listen here beloved, until your cabinets are completely bare, the only thing in your fridge is the light bulb and all that's left in the freezer is the ice tray, you have something to cook! Get on Al Gore's internet and find inspiration and recipes to repurpose your leftovers and create meals you didn't know existed from the ingredients you already have.

Here's a sobering fact…. According to National Resources Defense Council[12], 40% of the food grown, processed, and transported in the U.S. will never be eaten. This equates to 70 billion (yes BILLION) pounds of food that is lost annually. Even worse, nearly one-third of this food waste occurs because we purchase, cook, or serve more than we consume. LET'S NOT BE WASTEFUL. With some advanced planning and creativity, you can make tasty yet balanced, healthy meals that your entire family enjoys.

Once you've done all you can with your pre-existing ingredients, it's time to head to the supermarket. If you do need to grocery shop, meal plan, make a list of the items you need, then do an inventory BEFORE you shop.

As a child, I remember my mother making out the dinner menu for the week every Sunday. Mommy was big on planning and preparation. It set the tone and expectation for our household (we knew when she started on the menu, we had better be getting our clothes prepared for the week) and as a bonus, the Sunday paper had the biggest distribution of coupons for the week. She would see what we already had and then make out our shopping list based on that. Little did I realize she was teaching and training me on how to be efficient, effective and a conservationist. She was the queen of buying in bulk and then separating into smaller portions, from cereals to fresh and frozen produce and vegetables. This doubled as food prep and snack portions. WHO KNEW?!

The meats were no exception. I can remember my mother and grandmother purchasing their meats in bulk at a butcher/meat market (FYI…. each stroke of the knife in processing costs more at checkout; buy in bulk and do it yourself to cut the costs). Mommy also was an expert at seasonal shopping; she bought fruits and vegetables in season and then frozen or canned them for later. My amazing daddy introduced me to the wonderful world of gardening.

Over the years, I've built on what she's taught me. I now purchase my non-perishables and non-food products online. Amazon is not just for toys, electronics, and houseware. Products like protein bars and detergents are ideal for buying from online retailers like Amazon or your local store's online site. It saves you money because you won't have to pay food tax and if shipping is free, that's an added incentive. I also learned how to make my budget stretch by leveraging grocery outlets and day-old bakeries. You may be surprised at some real gems you find in these places for a fraction of the cost.

For my newbies to prepping and list shopping, a full week may seem like a daunting task so start with planning for 3 or 4 days and try to limit your shopping to only once a week. You'll tend to spend more if you stop at the store every day or several times a week. I promise you, the list is a lifesaver. It keeps your budget from inflating. And depending on your level of dedication to saving, you can use those weekly mailers (email or print) to plan out your grocery purchases for the week and take some time to compare prices for your favorite food from different stores. This helps prevent budget-busting impulse buys. Lastly, skip the BOGO (buy one, get one) sales. Either you'll end up purchasing foods you won't eat, or you'll pay an inflated price for the 'buy' item to cover the cost of the free/deeply discounted one.

TIP

- *Create leftovers purposefully.* If you prepare twice the vegetables you'll need for tonight's dinner, you'll have the starting point for a soup or pasta dish later in the week. Just don't forget to use it! Use leftover chicken on a sandwich. Convert the vegetable medley into a veggie fajita wrap. Turn leftover steak or pork into tacos. Cook twice as much rice as you need and freeze the extra for later use (p.s., the best fried rice is made with day-old rice, you're welcome!).

DAY 10

INVITE GOD INTO YOUR FINANCES

"Trust God from the bottom of your heart; don't try to figure out
everything on your own.
Listen for God's voice in everything you do, everywhere you go;
he's the one who will keep you on track.
~Proverbs 3:5 (MSG)

Personal finance books are hot sellers (you're reading one right now ☺). Bestselling authors like Dave Ramsey (Financial Peace), Tiffany Aliche (Get Good with Money), Paul Stanley (Millionaire Mindset), and Dr. Kate Levinson (Emotional Currency) provide excellent advice on how to manage finances and build a lasting legacy. Yet there is a book that is often overlooked and undervalued. Its popularity and solid financial guidance spans generations. You've guessed it: the Bible.

Of course, most people don't think of the Good Book as a personal finance guide. It's frequently viewed as a historical reference, the most revered body of literature and even the most impactful influence on humanity. But very few seek out the financial wisdom found in the Bible.

Several narratives and proverbs from the Bible, written thousands of years ago, demonstrate financial concepts that are as relevant as ever in the modern world. Did you know that there are over 2,300 Bible verses on, wealth, and possessions[13], yet many Christians aren't aware of exactly what God has to say about personal finances. In fact, most of us tend to leave God out of our money decisions, when the very Word of God should be primary when setting financial priorities. Look at a few principles found in the Bible:

- **Budgeting**

Luke 14:28-30 (AMPC) – "For which of you, wishing to build a farm building, does not first sit down and calculate the cost to see whether he has sufficient means to finish it? [29]Otherwise, when he has laid foundation and is unable to complete the building, all who see it will begin to mock and jeer at him, [30]Saying, This man began to build and was not able (worth enough) to finish."

It gets no clearer than this, people! Establishing a realistic budget prior to doing anything, especially a major feat like a construction project, is a critical component. Having a budget helps to keep your spending under control while moving towards your goals. Budgeting accounts for recurring expenses, one-time necessities, and contingencies, those unexpected emergencies. We will go into greater details later.

- **Avoid Debt**

Proverbs 22:7(MSG) – The poor are always ruled over by the rich, so don't borrow and put yourself under their power.

You don't need to be a Biblical scholar to understand the content and context of this scripture. In its simplistic form, we become enslaved by debt. The Pew Charitable Trusts substantiates this by saying that "...for many Americans, debt is a condition that lasts a lifetime and is impossible to escape[14]." If debt is not leveraged properly, this statement is true. Although there are ways to use debt to your advantage (build credit, accrue debt to grow your income and encourage wealth-building), many fall to debt's perceived power and control. Instead of you managing it, debt is managing you and dictating your financial moves. Some have even allowed debt to affect their physical and mental health; elevated levels of debt can be positively linked to migraines, digestive issues, high blood pressure, and immunodeficiencies as well as stress, marital problems, anxiety, depression, and even suicidal thoughts[15].

This same Pew report is showing a ray of hope for the Millennials. They are more aligned to the Biblical backdrop of debt; in that they more so see debt as burdensome than the perceived opportunistic vehicle society proclaims it to be. Their desire is to rid themselves of current debt and find resourceful ways of funding without debt lurking behind them.

- **Set Priorities**

Proverbs 24:27 (AMPC) – Put first things first. Prepare your work outside and get it ready for yourself in the field; and afterward build your house and establish a home.

In this passage, it lists the priority of work and the payoff for the arduous work. The field represents the farmer's livelihood, which then produces the essential resource for funding the house. Without the field being properly prepared, crops properly planted and tended to, and the crops harvested at the right time, how could the farmer make the money to build and maintain the house?

Albeit, farming is not as popular for generating income, the same principle applies today. To build and maintain household needs, most require some form of gainful employment. What good is a house if you don't have the means to put food on the table or pay the rent/mortgage?

Another bit of wisdom from this proverb is to set priorities with your money. Make sure you save enough to cover the essentials (build a house) before spending money on wants (establish a home).

- **Contingency Planning**

Genesis 41:34-36 (ESV) – Let Pharaoh proceed to appoint overseers over the land and take one-fifth of the produce of the land of Egypt during the seven plentiful years. [35] And let them gather all the food of these good years that are coming and store up grain under the authority of Pharaoh for food in the cities, and let them keep it. [36] That food shall be a reserve for the land against the seven years of famine that are to occur in the land of Egypt, so that the land may not perish through the famine."

In a nutshell, Joseph accurately interprets Pharaoh's dream, revealing that the seven fat cows symbolize seven years of prosperity for Egypt, and the seven lean cows represents seven years of famine that will immediately follow. In knowing what was coming, Joseph recommends that Pharaoh stockpile grain during the seven good years and use the stored grain to not only get the country through the seven hard years to follow but also use it as leverage to expand their real estate portfolio (read Genesis 47:19-20). In one of the first known plans for building an emergency fund and capitalizing on supply and demand, it demonstrates that saving is not just for a rainy day but also for opportunities that will arise to expand wealth!

Get into the practice of saving money when it is more readily available so you have it should times get lean. Look at the COVID Pandemic of 2020, the housing market crash (and subsequent recession) of 2008, and the recession of 1982, to name a few. But let's not limit savings preparation to impending global events. This preparation is inclusive of job loss, a health problem that could saddle you with hefty medical bills, and just plain ol' wise stewardship.

- **Diversified Portfolio**

Ecclesiastes 11:2 – Invest in seven ventures, yes, in eight; you do not know what disaster may come upon the land.

This verse from Ecclesiastes is a short, clear explanation of why it makes sense to diversify your investments. Any type of investment can fall victim to "evil" of some sort, whether it's a plague of locusts that wipes out a grain crop or a market crash that reduces the value of stocks or real estate. So, it makes sense to put money into many diverse types of investments so that a single disaster can't cost you everything you have.

- **Wise Stewardship**

Ephesians 5:15-16 (NIV) Be very careful, then, how you live—not as unwise but as wise, making the most of every opportunity, because the days are evil.

Many Christians struggle with the desire to live a financially comfortable lifestyle, giving to the Church and building wealth simultaneously. Some believe that if you are a Believer, then you're not supposed to be rich, as it implies that you love and lust after money more than you desire to please God. In their mind, God and money don't mix. We can debunk this oil and water mentality based on the above scripture. You can wisely pursue opportunities of financial gains while keeping the proper Biblical perspective, which is giving (it's held in a higher regard over gaining). If one of your desires is to give to programs like youth scholarship funds, cancer research foundations, and organizations that service seniors, then your mindset transcends gaining to solely to benefit you.

The overall Bible-money conversations reveals that money itself isn't bad – it's all in how you prioritize it in your life. Money should not be your sole focus. I get so turned off and quickly 'check out' of a conversation if the person is constantly talking about 'securing their bags.' Make these lessons from the Bible apart of your renewed mentality on money:

- The wealth you possess has been given by God.
- You are stewards of the resources He has provided.
- God cares about the way you handle finances.
- You should pursue excellence when it comes to money management.
- At no point should you care more about your wealth over your relationship with Christ.
- It is not sinful to have money.
- God values giving more than He values earning.

Remember, money should be wielded as a tool to do good; you must be intentional in how you handle it so that it will not drive a wedge between you and God, the One who provided it.

TIP

- Rather than obsessing about how much money you have and how you can make more, take some time to be grateful for what you already have. This is Biblical wisdom that can benefit even the most experienced investor.

DAY 11

THE BUDGET BATTLE

"A budget is telling your money where to go instead of wondering where it went."

~Dave Ramsey

At one point in my life, whenever I heard the word budget, I would immediately think, "that's just so restrictive. I can't live my life in a confined box." How insanely naïve was I? This classic avoidance behavior I engaged in was a mask to cover the factual issues. I was in pain financially but up to that point, had refused to address the root cause.

I did what I could to run from the pain instead of allowing the pain to help me. I didn't realize that pain and discomfort are good things. Yes, you heard me correctly. Pain is a good thing, for it's an indicator that something is off. It's a signal that something needs to be addressed before more damage is caused. Pain, discomfort, and discontentment are your cues to address the problem.

As one who had chronic back pain issues, I realize all too well how pain is communicated. People don't come with warning lights, like the lights on a car dashboard; you need the sensation of pain to let you know when your body needs extra care. It's an important signal. When your body is injured in some way or something else is wrong, your nerves send millions of messages to your brain about what's going on. Your brain then makes you feel pain. So, if you put your hand on a hot stove, your nerves call your brain, and your brain instantly sends the message that your hand hurts. You get this message and pull your hand away from the hot stove, which saves your hand from further injury. Pain helped you from further injuring yourself. If it didn't hurt to pull away from the hot stove, you might keep your hand there, causing more damage.

Pain is a protective reaction. However, if you continue ignoring pain signals and hurt yourself, it could cause nerve damage, thus sending faulty communication to your brain. Damaged nerves can send signals when there is no bodily distress or not send signals when there is bodily distress. Financial pain can mirror bodily pain. As with the body, faulty financial signals can communicate "go ahead and pamper yourself with a massage, manicure, and pedicure. You've had a rough week and required some much-needed self-care to protect your peace" when you know you don't have enough to cover your car payment and mortgage.

I learned to embrace the pain. I tapped in and allowed the financial pain and discomfort to communicate what was going on with my finances. I stopped avoiding the issues, took the mask off and got real with myself. The added motivation to become more disciplined was that I was no longer working, as my traditional income was no longer there to support me. With my safety net and comfort zone now gone, what choice did I have but to work on me?

The pain was the fruit, but I had to get to and expose the root of the pain. Just as medical professionals ask questions to help understand the source of the pain, so too did I begin to ask myself questions to help find the underlying cause of my financial woes. As Suze Oman says, "the only way you will ever permanently take control of your financial life is to dig deep and fix the root problem." Most of the time, your problems don't stem from just one thing, but rather several layered issues working in tandem.

At my former job, I collaborated with teams to help with continuous improvement and quality. One technique that I found particularly useful in uncovering issues was the 5 Whys technique. This amazing yet simplistic technique repeatedly asks "why" to drill down to the real cause of nearly any problem. Its goals are to discover the root cause of a problem, fully understand how to fix, compensate, or learn from any underlying issues within the root cause, and thirdly apply what you learn from this analysis to prevent future issues or to repeat successes.

You start by writing down the problem you are having, as it helps make the issue tangible and confronts any denial that might keep you from moving forward. Then you would ask 'why' the problem exists. Next ask 'why' again to that response. Repeat the 'whys' until the root cause(s) become evident.

To illustrate this technique, let's take on why you have not written that book yet ☺ .

1. Why haven't you written the book?
   - I work 16 hours a day.
2. Why do you work 16 hours a day?
   - I need the extra money
3. Why do you need extra money?

- I need to get out of debt

4. Why are you in debt?

- I spend too much money

5. Why do you spend so much money?

- I feel sad and depressed and shopping helps me feel better

From this example, you can see the feelings of depression and sadness cause a chain reaction that eventually prevents this person from fulfilling their purpose.

I did a '5 whys' of my budgeting blues. I discovered that my avoidance was really rooted in feelings of inadequacy, which led to spending. So, the plan was to address the spending (fruit) as well as the inadequate feelings (root), which stemmed from work and relationships (more like the lack thereof). Through prayer, therapy, mentorship, and an accountability partner, I learned how to rid myself of unhelpful comparisons, constant self-criticism, poor coping habits, and unrealistic expectations. This is ongoing work for me.

In addition to my internal healing and the spending moratorium, I began making a plan for my money by knowing what's going out and coming in monthly. I started out using a simple Excel spreadsheet, listing out every bill that I had to pay. Because I'm such a detailed person, I included the due date, payoff amount, interest rate and date the debt was incurred. Eventually, I started using the app TrueBill, as it gave me the mobile convenience and trackability from my phone.

Budget Battle

The budget was not a one-and-done thing; I reviewed my budget monthly, as each month was not the same. There were birthdays, anniversaries, holidays, back to school, and other events that had to be accounted for in their respective months. For the first time, I felt like I finally had control over my money. I was now telling it what to do and where to go. Nothing was left to chance. Before the month was done, I was reviewing and preparing for the next month. Truth be told, I started enjoying doing this!

Unfortunately, the word *budget* has gotten a bad rap, and had a bad connotation with me. A budget is the key to financial health—there's no way around it. If you don't keep track of where your money is going and where it *should* be going, it won't take much for spending to get out of control.

When it all boils down, a budget is just a plan for your money. Budgeting means you're spending with purpose *before* the month begins. Unfortunately, many people view a budget as a straitjacket (LIKE ME!) that will keep them from doing what they want. But that couldn't be further from the truth! *A budget doesn't limit your freedom—it gives you freedom!* It's really all about being intentional with where your money goes.

Currently, there's a popular phrase our culture loves to post on social media....I DON'T KNOW WHO NEEDS TO HEAR THIS... to avoid directly speaking to a person or situation. I KNOW WHO NEEDS TO HEAR THIS....YOU SIS, YOU, MY BROTHER! I'M TALKING TO YOU!

Many want to become millionaires but cannot handle the budget of being hundredaires or thousandaires. When you become faithful over what has been entrusted to you, you will get more. Tough love moment...You are your biggest hinderance; you are your own warfare because you lack self-restraint. Stop spending. Get wisdom. Become disciplined.

Right here, right now, you are going to make a different decision. You ARE going to face the issues, get to the root cause and take control of your spending through budgeting. You will NOT overextend your finances due to a lack of discipline. You will no longer be in the red (deficit) but always be in the black (surplus).

I am choosing to speak life over you and your finances. Now to those words of affirmation, let's add some action. There's no need to be intimidated by what may seem like a tedious task, either. There are plenty of resources out there to help you budget.

With my first budget, I used three simple steps:

1. List all sources of income and the amount. Whether it's through a traditional job, 1099 work, child support, or passive income from residuals or property, it needs to be listed.

2. List every expense (monthly and seasonal). This is where most of the groundwork happens. I used my bank and credit card statements over a six-month period. I'm extreme! You can start off with two months.

3. Subtract expenses from income. If you have extra left over, apply it towards paying off your debt or into savings! If you get a negative number, you will need to cut back on something or pick up extra work to cover it. Refer to Day 16, Additional Streams of Income.

For my techies, there's great news: there's an app for that… Many, to be specific. If you're looking to take and keep control of your finances, you can manage the process from your phone or tablet as easily as you can check email, send a Tweet or post on IG.

Once you have the fundamentals locked down and integrated into your budgeting routine, you've already done a lot of the hard work of getting into financial shape. It's never too early to start planning for 'later'—including retirement and building a legacy for the next generation. And it doesn't have to be scary; if you make good money habits part of your daily and weekly routines, you can help avoid (some of) the pinches of adulting.

When it comes to budgeting, Dave Ramsey became the money mentor in my head I never knew I needed. I started by listening to his broadcasts on my lunch break, then purchased his books and finally enrolled in his program. This was one of the greatest investments I made in myself and my lineage. His no-nonsense, tough love approach got me all the way together. Between his tools and my trial and errors, below you will find some practical applications and pitfalls to avoid.

1. Invite God into your finances.

Pray and ask for His wisdom to help guide you, His grace to cover you and, His insight to show you things about yourself that may be affecting your finances.

2. Do your budget EVERY month.

Each month may be different when you factor in birthdays, anniversaries, car maintenance, etc.

3. Budget to zero before the month begins.

This means before the month even starts, you're planning to give every dollar a name. It's called a zero-based budget. Now that doesn't mean you have zero dollars in your bank account. It just means your income minus all your expenses equals zero.

4. Couples, discuss and do the budget together.

With money being one of the main reasons why couples divorce, it is imperative that married couples talk about and plan their financial lives together. Praying together regarding your finances will take it to a greater level.

5. Get aggressive with paying off debt.

This means you may need to tighten the belt and trim the fat. No more 15-word coffee drinks from the specialty shop, no vacation abroad for a year, manicures and pedicures are now done at home, maybe it's time to get rid of cable (you already have 5 subscriptions to different entertainment apps anyways!). When paying off debt, consider using either the Snowball or Highest Interest Rate Method.

a) The Snowball Method. This method concentrates on paying down the debt with the least balance while maintaining minimum payments on all other debts. Once the smallest balance is paid off, apply those funds you were paying on your smallest debt toward the next smallest balance, building momentum, or "snowballing" your repayment toward the next balance. This cycle repeats until all your debt is paid.

b) Highest Interest Rate Method. This method is primarily aimed at debt like credit cards and student loans and others with the highest rate of interest. The goal is to pay off the highest interest rate debt as quickly as possible since it's eating up most of your budget. Although you may not experience the quick wins that the Snowball Method affords you, this method eliminates your highest debts first—which saves you money in the long run.

6. Track your progress.

It's important to check your progress from time to time. If you're married, get together and regularly talk about your goals.

7. Proactively plan for contingencies.

Preemptive preparations will keep you from 'robbing Peter to pay Paul.' Create a cushion in your costs by way of an emergency fund. If you haven't done so already, start with saving $1,000, then transition to saving the equivalent of three months of your household expenses, and finally save six months of expenses.

Label the savings as your miscellaneous category in your budget (remember, every dollar is being allocated to budget to zero) so that if an emergency arises, you don't have to play Checkers (moving money around from another category) to cover the unexpected expense. If this expense becomes a recurring theme, it's time to move it to a more permanent line item in your budget.

8.   Cash is king!

Let's be honest, lack of discipline landed you here. Until you can manage your credit cards, meaning having a zero balance by month's end, it's time you dump the plastic AND deactivate them from your online accounts. Having no credit card debt will mean no more minimum payments to add to the budget. Stick to using your debit card and cash.

9.   Goals and Grace.

Do set your financial goals (I recommend adding a vision board) and actively work towards them but give yourself some grace if you don't hit the bullseye with every goal.

TIP

- If you're planning to go out, or have regular nights out, make sure you work this into your budget for the week/month, so that you don't find yourself scrambling to cover other things when the credit card payment is due. Things like going out with friends can make your expenses snowball. When you're out and about, it's so easy to lose track of what you're spending and where. Keep your receipts to compare to what you allocated for that night. It's all about holding yourself accountable.

DAY 12

SAVING FOR OPPORTUNITIES, NOT JUST A RAINY DAY

"Don't save what is left after spending. Spend what is left after saving."

~Warren Buffet

So often, we are conditioned to save in preparation for a storm, but I am challenging you to shift your mindset to think "I am saving for opportunities that are coming." Prepare for the best not the worst. By saving, you are in a financial position to capitalize on the presented opportunity. From purchasing a business, real estate investment, or stocks to simply helping someone else, you will have the means to effortlessly do so.

Although saving a portion of your income and investing in a 401k program are two of the most popular ways to amass savings, let's explore other options to build your savings.

1. Review your cell phone plans
2. Review your cable TV packages
3. Review your insurance plans
4. Opt for a staycation.
5. Skip the 10-word specialty coffee drink.
6. Stop smoking.
7. Disconnect your cards from online shopping sites and food delivery services.

8. Cook instead of going out to eat.

9. Stop the gym membership.

10. Change light bulbs to energy efficient bulbs.

11. Buy generic.

12. Set up auto deposit into your savings (through job or through your bank).

13. DIY your next home project.

14. Couponing.

15. Turn your thermostat down 7-10 degrees for eight hours daily.

16. Grocery shop on Wednesdays (most retailers launch new sales midweek).

17. Unsubscribe to email subscriptions from retail stores.

18. Leverage the library for free entertainment (books, movies, classes)

19. Volunteer at a festival or concert (you attend free of charge).

20. Weatherproof your home.

21. Review tax benefits. One of the worst pains is knowing you 'left money on the table,' meaning you did not maximize on an opportunity. One such opportunity is lowering your tax bill or increased your tax refund on your tax return. Here are some tax deductions that you shouldn't overlook.

    o   Sales taxes

    o   Health insurance premiums

    o   Tax savings for educators

    o   Charitable gifts and donations

    o   Paying the babysitter

Saving

- o Lifetime learning credit
- o Unusual business expenses
- o Looking for work
- o Self-employed social security
- o Reinvested dividends
- o Student loan interest paid by you or someone else
- o Moving expenses
- o State tax you paid last spring
- o Refinancing mortgage points
- o Jury pay paid to employer
- o Saving for college
- o Home sale
- o Tax loss harvesting (you sell an investment that has lost money)
- o Investment fees and expenses
- o Disaster recovery deduction
- o Medical expenses
- o Child and dependent care credit

TIP

- Time your purchases. If you can wait, the best time to purchase is during an 'end of season' sale.

DAY 13

Consider Going Cash-Only.

"Three of the most dreaded words in the English language is 'negative cash flow.'"

~David Tang

If you are having difficulty remaining consistent to your budget and eliminating credit card spend, it may be time to consider switching to cash-only. It helps to avoid temptation and increase financial accountability. That way, your credit card balances stay intact for emergencies, and you're less likely to overspend.

There is a level of convenience that comes with credit cards, especially when emergencies arise, and you need to cover a large expense immediately. However, they're also kind of the devil… tempt you to do wrong then mock you for doing wrong. "Charge it," they whisper from your wallet. "Buy it now, you have plenty of time to pay it later. Live it up, my friend!" A year later, that dress and girls' night out is still racking up interest because you can only afford to pay the minimum payment.

Although everything can't be paid in cash (car payment, mortgage, student loan), there are still plenty of items that can be. All your entertainment, groceries, gasoline, utilities, and shopping are cash expenditures.

Cash Only!

One of the most effective cash-only systems is one that I learned from Dave Ramsey, the envelope system. This simplistic method empowers you to remain true to your spending; it limits (once the money is gone, that's it for the month) and tracks your spend by keeping the receipts in the respective envelopes.

1. To begin, you'll need to create your budget for the month (each month will be different; refer to Day 11).

2. Determine what portion of your budget will be discretionary spending (i.e., eating out, groceries, clothes, gasoline, dry cleaning, entertainment).

3. Go to the bank (yes, I know, who does that anymore!) and withdraw the total amount. Get the denominations broken down in such a way that you can put the correct amount in each envelope.

4. Organize your envelopes for each category by labeling them with the categories and allotted spend for the month. Store the envelopes in a secure space in your home.

5. When you engage in the respective envelope's activity, take out the money you need (hopefully it's not the entire amount in the envelope) for that one outing.

6. Once done, review the receipts in that envelope to see your spend that month.

TIP

- Do not "borrow" from other envelopes if you run out of money from one of your envelopes; once it's gone, it's gone.

DAY 14

REDUCE DEBT TO INCOME RATIO

"Debts are like children: the smaller they are the more noise they make."

-Spanish Proverb

If you are honest, sometimes it's hard to persist when you're struggling financially. This is especially true when you don't see the returns on the changes you've made to get out of debt. Your credit score is stagnant, even with all your diligent work. The balances do not seem to be decreasing fast enough. Here's where I'm going to give you some tough love…. ***But what other option do you really have?*** You must be intentional in creating and sustaining momentum; put the pedal to the metal and don't stop anymore. That's what it takes to get to your financial destination.

Bravo for doing the work. This is certainly something to be happy about. In all your fervent work to be debt free, have you considered your debt-to-income (DTI) ratio? This critical number tells you the percentage of your gross monthly income that goes toward paying your debt. Many lenders, especially mortgage and auto lenders, use your debt-to-income ratio to determine if you are living within your means and can afford to incur another debt based on your income.

You can easily calculate your debt-to-income ratio using this formula:

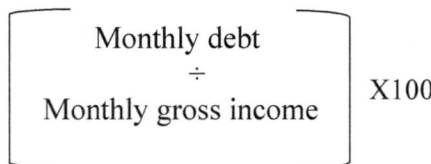

1. Total Your Monthly Debt

The first step in calculating your debt-to-income ratio is determining how much you spend each month on debt. To start, add up the total amount of your monthly debt payments, including the following:

- Mortgage or rent
- Minimum credit card payments
- Car loan
- Student loans
- Alimony/child support payments
- Other loans or lines of credit

Note: You don't need to include payments you make for car insurance, utilities, health insurance, groceries, and other monthly expenses, as these are not reported to the credit bureaus.

2. Total Your Monthly Income

Next, calculate your monthly income by adding up all amounts you receive each month.:

- Gross income from a W-2 job or self-employment
- Bonuses or overtime
- Alimony/child support

Debt-to-Income Ratio

- Other income from various sources

Note: Multiply your weekly income by four and bi-monthly income by two to calculate your total monthly income. Or, if you know your annual salary, divide it by twelve to get to your monthly income.

Example

For example, my monthly debt payments total $7,829 and my monthly income totals $33,675. So, divide $7,829 by $33,675 and then multiply by 100:

$7,829 ÷ $33,675 = 0.2324 X 100 = 23.2%

I have a debt-to-income ratio of 23.2%.

What Your Debt-to-Income Ratio Means[16]

o **36%** or **less** is the healthiest debt load for most people. If your debt-to-income ratio falls within this range, avoid incurring more debt to maintain a good ratio.

o **37%** to **42%** isn't a bad ratio to have, but it could be better. If your ratio falls in this range, you should start reducing your debts. You may have trouble getting approved for a mortgage within this range.

o **43%** to **49%** is a ratio that indicates financial trouble. You should start aggressively paying your debts to prevent an overloaded debt situation.

o **50%** or **more** is an extremely dangerous ratio. This means that more than half of your income goes toward debt payments each month.

Knowing is half the battle, so how do you reach "Destination Manifestation?" Let's look at opportunities to help you stay the course to reduce your debt-to-income ratio.

1. Lower your credit card interest rate. Call the holding companies and ask for a lower rate. It costs you nothing to do it and what's the worst they'll say? STOP TELLING YOURSELF NO AND QUIT TALKING YOURSELF OUT OF IT.

2. Review all things associated with your home and mortgage.

    i. Refinance your mortgage. As of today (Jan 2022), interest rates are extremely low. Refi to lock in a lower interest rate and take some of your equity to pay down your bills.

    ii. Modify your mortgage. This is more of a streamlined version of refinancing. Once you pay the modification fee, you can reduce your interest rate without requalifying. It is much less cumbersome than the traditional refinance and does not have unfavorable effects.

    iii. Negotiate your real estate taxes. If your home is being assessed for a lesser value, go to your tax assessor and request for an adjusted assessment, which results in lowered real estate taxes.

iv.   Review your homeowners' insurance. You may find a better deal.

v.   Get rid of PMI. Is it a tax deduction, yes, but the most advantageous path would be positioning yourself to not have this built into your mortgage. Connect with your lender and see how you can qualify for removal.

vi.   Whether buying or selling, negotiate the price. If buying, don't be afraid to ask for 10% below the value. Depending on their counteroffer, you can add in immediate costs and repairs that arise from the home inspection, if your numbers are supported by reasonable data. Look at the age of cabinets, windows, furnace, water heaters and deduct if it's old. Also ask the seller to pay closing costs / mortgage points. If savvy enough, skip using a real estate agent, which can save 3%.

vii. Turn your home (partial or the whole home) into a rental. Either having a roommate or renting a space like the basement can help alleviate expenses and help subsidize your mortgage payment. If you are near a major venue or event, you can rent out your house for up to two weeks tax-free.

viii. Negotiate repairs and improvements. SHOP AROUND! Get multiple quotes and negotiate. Typically, the first offer is the worst offer.

3. Shop around for insurance. Companies will compete for your business.

4. Review your subscriptions. More about this on Day 15.

5. Make biweekly payments. In doing this, you will make 13 payments for the year, removing nearly five years of payments on a 30-year mortgage. The same can be done for car payments and credit card payments (this can appear to be two monthly payments, which helps your credit score).

6. Barter and trade things and services with others (you know how to do hair, she knows how to do nails, trade services). If the pandemic of 2020 taught us nothing else, it taught us to be imaginative, resourceful, ingenious and reinvent our norms.

7. Get out of debt using the Snowball or Largest Interest Rate Method. We discussed this in depth on Day 11.

8. Learn the art of the deal – NEGOTIATE. It's a tool that will serve you well at every step of your professional and personal life. Negotiate to increase your pay and benefits. It's not just about a better biweekly salary; also consider a signing bonus, a review at 6 months, flexible work schedule, paid time off, relocation expenses, your title, professional development. Negotiate to get a better deal on your car. You can negotiate the price of your home (especially new construction), from covering HOA fees and closing cost to upgraded finishes. The sky is the limit; you just need to be your best advocate.

9. BUDGETING – STICK TO IT. We just discussed this on Day 11!

10. Create a passive income with a side business. Common ways people earn passive income include creating blogs, becoming a social media influencer (approximately one billion hours of YouTube videos are watched daily[17], so there's an audience for you!) are just a few potential income earners. While it may cost you time and creativity, the payout has the potential to be great (depending on your level of effort and the market interest). More about this on Day 16.

11. Look into your current employee benefits. Many companies offer benefits that enable you to save money, such as flexible spending

account (FSA) and 401(k) options. These benefits help lower the amount of income taxed, thus you see a larger take-home pay.

12. Modify your tax withholdings from your paycheck. This will immediately increase your income. Just be aware that you will still be accountable for paying taxes on your income at the end of the year.

13. Increase your career capital by earning a certification. Pursuing a certification can increase the income earned in certain careers.

14. Ask for a raise or promotion. Conversely, consider applying for a different role.

15. Drive for a rideshare company. If you have a reliable vehicle and a clean driving record, you can drive for the likes of Uber or Lyft.

16. GO GREEN. How does going green save money? Going green doesn't have to be expensive or time-consuming. Listed below[18] are some recommendations to save money by going green, with little to no investment.

   a) Replace your appliances. Example: Your current refrigerator may operate on 1,000 kWh per year. A newer, more energy efficient refrigerator uses just 100 kWh per year. At $0.12 per kWh, your old fridge costs you $120 in energy per year versus $12 with the new refrigerator.

b) Unplug appliances that are not in use. Example: Shutting down and unplugging appliances such as your computer (unplug, not put to sleep or power off), coffee pot, cable box, DVD players, sound bars, etc. can deliver an annual savings between $100 and $200.

c) Make smart food choices - Example: Store-bought tomatoes cost about $2 per pound. A tomato plant in your garden will cost about $10, including the seeds, soil, water, and fertilizer. That plant can deliver about ten pounds of tomatoes. Use a rain barrel to collect the rain and water the garden. This will save on water usage.

d) Skip single-use products – Example: Paper towel rolls cost $14 per eight-pack, and the average family spends about $182 per year on those towels. Dish towels, on the other hand, cost about $6, and it's a one-time investment.

e) Save on water – Example: A bath requires 36 gallons of water. A five-minute shower requires just ten gallons. A gallon of water costs about $0.01, so swapping out baths for showers could save $0.25 per day, nearly $100 annually.

f) Reassess your commute – Example: Owning a car costs a family about $8,500 per year. Owning a bike cost just $350 per year. Some people (me....I am some people!) may not have the comfort level of riding a bike to work, so there is public transportation and carpool for your consideration. Any method you can use to cut back on solo trips will save you money and help the environment.

g) Join the sharing economy – Example: A rental wedding dress costs about $775 per day. Buying a similar dress could cost you anywhere from $2,000 to $13,000.

h) Cut your energy bill – Example: BC Hydro suggests that 90% of washing machine energy goes toward heating the water. By switching to cold, you could save approximately $5 per month.

i) Sell your gently used clothes and other items online. We talked about this on Day 6. You can also go to thrift stores in your spare time to find gently used designer items and list these as well to make a profit.

17. Use Fiverr to source gigs. No matter what service you are providing, Fiverr offers a home to all freelancers, from graphic and web designer to bloggers, ghostwriters, accountants, and so on. Anything you can imagine that's legal can be procured and sold as a service on Fiverr.

18. If you are crafty, upcycle! Purchase items from Flea Markets and secondhand stores, redesign, and sell them for major profits.

Don't feel the need to do all of these at one time. Make a commitment to try one change at a time and track your progress. As your savings grow and your costs dip, you'll get motivated to do even more.

TIP

- Stop taking on more debt. Don't apply for a new credit, avoid running up your current credit card balances, and delay any major purchases.

DAY 15

GIVE YOURSELF A RAISE

"Change will not come if we wait for some other person or some other time. We are the ones we've been waiting for. We are the change that we seek."

~ Barack Obama

With utility bills, credit cards, loan payments, subscriptions, memberships, and other recurring monthly expenses, it's nearly impossible to keep track of all those due dates in your head. In comes mobile apps to save the day. Personal finance apps aren't just limited to helping you budget. They can also track your spending so you can see where all your money is going and point out spending categories where you might be able to cut back. Some budgeting apps can monitor subscriptions and remind you of payment due dates, too. I absolutely love Truebill for this very reason.

In addition to monitoring my spending, receiving weekly notifications of what is due that week, and credit score/report monitoring, I can also manage my subscriptions in the app, cancelling what I no longer want. (PayPal also allows you to manage subscriptions if you selected PayPal as your method of payment. For my team iPhone users, you can manage subscriptions associated with your Apple ID through your device.)

Subscriptions are a fantastic way to get the products and services you want on a regular basis. Yet, some people (me, I am some people) find themselves spending more money than they anticipated on their subscriptions. Here are all the subscriptions I had before my spending fast:

1. Netflix	12. Audible	27. DoorDash
2. Hulu	13. Sirius XM	28. GrubHub
3. Apple TV	14. Apple Music	29. UberEats
4. BET+	15. Discovery+	30. Postmates
5. Allblk	16. Shutterstock	31. Instacart
6. Epix	17. AdoreMe	32. Ring Central
7. HBOMax	18. FentyxSavage	33. eFax
8. KevOnStageStudios	19. Amazon Prime	34. Zoom
	20. ShoeDazzle	35. Adobe Creative
9. Patreon for KevOnStage	21. JustFab	36. MS Windows
	22. Rocket Lawyer	37. GoDaddy
10. Patreon for Jonathan McReynolds	23. Legal Zoom	38. VistaPrint
	24. Keto Diet	39. Compassion International
	25. BetterMe	
11. Amazon Prime Music	26. HookedOnPhoenics	40. Shopify

Yes, your girl was out of control. Because these were auto debited on different days throughout the month, I did not see or feel the impact until I did a 6-month review of my spending. My review showed I was being double charged for a few subscriptions and was incurring ongoing charges for some that I canceled. In canceling the unused and not-needed subscriptions, I gave myself a "raise," in that I gained $376 each month. This equates to $188 biweekly, or $4.70/hour. THAT'S MAJOR!!! For some, this would be a welcomed raise at work.

To avoid the cardinal mistake I made, take time to regularly review your subscriptions; my recommendation is to do it quarterly after you've made your initial assessment. Decide if your subscriptions are still fit for purpose: how often do you use the service, does it fit your budget, is it a duplicate of another service you have, can you get by without it. If you do indeed use the service, see if there is a lower-tiered service available.

TIP

- Watch out for cancellation or early termination fees. If you cancel a subscription that charges a fee, wait until you can do so without a penalty.

DAY 16

FINANCIAL FREEDOM. REAL #LifeGoals.

"To achieve what 1% of the world's population has (Financial Freedom), you must be willing to do what only 1% dare to do... hard work and perseverance of the highest order."
~ Manoj Arora

What would being financially free look like to you? Is it the ability to do whatever you want? Is it being independent of a traditional 9 to 5 job? Is it having millions of dollars at your disposal?

Many of you have gone to school or put in the work to develop and define the career you've want. You've either become or are well on your way to being identified as a:

Game changer

Rain maker

World shaker

Ceiling breaker

Yet, there is a sense brewing inside of you saying, "There is more." You've worked hard and the press and grind came at a price, one that you may no longer be willing to pay. You've made major sacrifices of your time with family and friends to the tune of having little time for yourself or time to enjoy the spoils of war from your success. Some of you are

95

exhausted at the end of the day, dragging yourselves to bed to prepare for another day like the last one.

Yes, you defied the odds but that model for working long hours, sacrificing family, friends, and yourself is no longer sustainable. If you really tap in and honestly evaluate yourself, you may realize it's time to start living the life you've always dreamed of, on your terms, in your timing.

Tough love moment....stop hiding behind a 9-to-5, making someone else richer and become an indispensable solution to others, with you at the helm the ship. Your expertise, experience, and aptitude are bigger than what you've been sharing on the job. You have the power to get wealth. Don't talk yourself out of it. Don't allow an imposter syndrome to make you think you can't do it. You are enough. You are the person for the job.

Some of you may be wondering why you are not at peace, even with the great successes you've experienced in your career. You have a nagging feeling in your gut that won't go away. Could it be that there is something more that you should be doing? There is something else that God has called you to do beyond the job, as your job may not be the sole venue for you to fully release your gifts and talents.

So, the question remains....what does life look like if you lived them on your terms? This is about you becoming a financially free person, in whatever capacity you choose. And that's really the key: it needs to be defined by you. So many people outsource this responsibility to others....society, social influencers, celebrities, family, friends... and consequently, never achieve it.

Take control of your dream, be the gate keeper of your vision. You are officially responsible for your happiness and the manager of your freedom. Begin to identify what financial freedom looks like for you, and then build a road map to do just that.

I am not going to preach to you and sell you some snake oil, promising you a "money-back guarantee" if it doesn't work in 30 days. You must define your own vision, develop your own strategy, and walk your own path. This is about the realization of just how great you are, what may be hindering you from living your best life and how to successfully break through those barriers.

Personally, financial freedom is not *HAVING* to work a 9-to-5 job to help support my family or using that job to assign my value, worth and validation. Financial freedom is the ability to share my gifts, talent, wisdom, and experience to enhance the quality of life of others, without consideration of how much I will make doing it. Financial freedom is being able to vacation when and how I want. It's the ability to retire at 45, should I choose. Financial freedom is leaving a diversified inheritance of stocks, property, businesses, and personal possessions to four generations beyond my husband and me. It is the ability to purchase my parents a home with a smile as we write a check for the full amount (after negotiating of course).

With the steady incline of unhappiness and unfulfillment in the workplace, something must change. Sadness, anxiety, loss of motivation, difficulty concentrating, unexplained bouts of crying, and boredom are just a small sample of the things you may be feeling if you're experiencing depressive symptoms at work. This workplace depression is largely due to feeling trapped, unable to realize potential and being denied opportunity. According to a survey conducted by Mental Health America [19], 83 percent of the 5,000 respondents felt emotionally drained from work and 71 percent said that the workplace affects their mental health. The data also showed that the number of people seeking help for depression increased significantly from 2019 to 2020. There was a 62 percent increase in people who took the survey's depression screen — and of those people, 8 in 10 tested positive for symptoms of moderate to severe depression.

When you consider that most full-time employees spend an average of 8.5 hours per day working on weekdays and 5.5 hours working on weekends and holidays, according to the Bureau of Labor Statistics [20] many will experience symptoms of depression while on the jo, since this is where they spend the bulk of their time. With these sobering statistics, it comes as no surprise that people are actively seeking strategies to meet their financial needs independent of a job.

You may not be in the population that experiences workplace stress or depression. Your fulfillment and balance could be everything you've desired and has provided a comfortable level of financial freedom for you. Congratulations on finding your place of peace and contentment. For those who are not here, let's put the work in to get you to a steady state of fulfillment, stability, and financial freedom.

For starters, ask yourself, "If money was not a need, what would I be doing?" What would life look like if I weren't constrained by a strict budget when making purchases? The stress and depression that comes from feeling like a 'wage-slave' is rooted in the absence of a clear picture of what you want. It is easy, and almost automated, to divert your attention to what you lack. This cycle perpetuates a mindset of lack that very quickly is reflected in your reality and further solidified by the images and conversations of what you don't have and what you can't do.

Many are commercially conditioned to believe that attaining financial freedom is achievable with millions of dollars. Although this is partly true, it's not the most accurate picture. It really does not take millions to establish financial freedom. After setting *your* expectations and standard of *your* financial freedom, then assess your current financial situation to see where you would have to be to gain freedom. For me, my primary classification of financial freedom is independence of a 9-to-5 job to sustain me. With that, I would need enough funds to exceed my monthly expenses. Oversimplified, yes, but that's where we need to start.

In its most simplistic form, if you can generate income (without going to a traditional job) that surpasses your monthly expenses, would you consider this financial freedom? According to my definition, ABSOLUTELY! Keep in mind, *my goal* is not about living an extravagant, extreme lifestyle. The goal is my ability to meet all my

99

financial obligations without having to work. I aspire to free up more time to fulfill my purpose and follow my dreams.

Bringing it back home....**WHAT DOES FINANCIAL FREEDOM LOOK LIKE FOR YOU**? What would your life be like on a day-to-day basis? What would you be doing? How would you feel? Where would you be? Sometimes a visual representation helps to paint the picture for your mind. Vision boards, video clips, pictures and any other media can help build a mental image. What are you doing to curate those opportunities and connections that will allow financial freedom?

While on your way to freedom, don't neglect or depreciate your current work situation. Whether you love or loathe your job, I challenge you to now look at it as a means to transition from work to independent wealth. While transitioning, do not get stuck, allow the job to define you or chip away at your desires.

TIP

- Ask yourself, "Would I be fulfilled working here if I didn't need the money."

DAY 17

ADDITIONAL STREAMS OF INCOME

"Compound interest is the eighth wonder of the world. He who
understands it, earns it.
He who doesn't, pays it."
~Albert Einstein

I believe it is safe to say that America is a proverbial land of 'milk and honey,' with its limitless opportunities to prosper and grow wealth. Research has shown:

- The U.S. accounts for 30% of global wealth, or $126.3 trillion.[21]
- The U.S. has the most millionaires (21.2 million) [22] and billionaires (724) [23] in the world.
- With infinite possibilities for achieving financial success, the U.S. inherits more than a million immigrants annually.[24]

On a global level, the world's total net wealth has hit $431 trillion, nearly half a quadrillion dollars[25]. Celebrating at the high end of this earning spectrum, billionaires have seen their fortunes soar in 2021. Forbes' annual report of billionaires listing for 2021 list now includes 2,755 billionaires (660 more than 2020), who collectively grew their wealth from $8 trillion in 2020 to $13.1 trillion in 2021[26]. This is during the height of the COVID-19 global pandemic. Looks like other people have plans for your money. You'd be smart to ensure YOU have a plan for YOUR money!

At some point in your lifetime, you've wondered, "well how did these millionaires and billionaires get to their financial status? How does the rich keep getting richer?" The truth is, millionaires and billionaires are no different than anyone else. The reason they produce so much wealth is because they have multiple income streams.

It has been shown that the rich have multiple streams of income to insulate their wealth. On average, they have seven income streams, while the bulk of middle class only have one income stream[27]. It's like saying the middle-class person works one job, while millionaires work seven jobs. The difference between those who are rich and those who aren't is largely based on a mindset. If you recall your 'coming of age' years, consider the words of wisdom that came from your parents, teachers and those who influenced you.

> *"Get an education.*
> *Excel academically.*
> *Distinguish yourself from others by joining organizations*
> *and becoming a leader.*
> *Work one or more internships.*
> *Network and secure a wonderful job that pays well*
> *and provides good benefits and a bonus."*

You see, most people are not being conditioned to think beyond a 9-to-5, yet alone bred to become a millionaire. They are pre-programmed to find a job. Many people are not even exposed to the other avenues to earn income and secure wealth. Real estate acquisitions, stock market investments, business ownership, writing for yourself or others are just a few of the many ways you can use to add to your income, yet these are not considered by most; the evidence is the high number of people who solely depend on their job to sustain their present and support their future. I'm not telling you to walk off your job. I am advocating for you to explore and expand beyond your career comfort zone.

Multiple streams help to ensure that you can maintain your lifestyle even if something happens to one of your sources of income. Diversifying your portfolio to include multiple revenue streams is the best way to achieve this goal and is something that everyone should consider. Frankly put, multiple streams are not optional if your end goal is building wealth and providing generational financial security.

With the understanding that time is money, and you have a limited amount of time each day to work, spend time with family, give back to others, and take care of yourself, it is essential to get out of the traditional mindset of trading hours for dollars; this is a limiting way of generating income. To your active income (your day-to-day job), passive income can help free your time while increasing your wealth. Passive income is money you don't have to do anything to continue to generate it. It provides a level of comfort because you are steadily producing income, even while you sleep, and since you sleep for eight hours a day, that's eight hours' worth of income you are generating by working smarter not harder.

Many pray for more money or a different career but are unwilling to use their talents and gifts to produce more. On Day 16, I discussed financial freedom. One of the greatest ways of securing financial freedom is through multiple streams of income. Whether it's investments, opening your business, or having a side gig, you can increase your income while sharing your gifts and talents with others.

Listed below are the most common streams of income. As with anything, doing your due diligence on risk and reward is paramount. Count the cost of your time, talent, and treasure before counting the bags you stand to gain!

1. Business Income

Business income is about trading a product or service for money. It refers to profits made from running an enterprise. A good example of business income is my eCommerce business Grace Gear, where we offer inspirational T-shirts, Scribe Publications, where we publish books for new and existing authors, conduct workshops, trainings, courses and much more, and our travel business JQ Travel .

If you can find a valuable product or service to offer to the marketplace, you can generate more income while helping others. With knowledge being the gateway to empowerment, people will pay for knowledge. Whether it's knowledge in food and beverage, logistics, training and development, real estate, an idea, concept, invention, or your life experiences, you have something in you that deserves to be unearthed, that deserves to be seen, worthy of being heard. Some may need to author a book, develop a mentorship program, create programs for youth, curate a cookbook, develop a screenplay. Decide that you are going to move from being a consumer to being a creator and producer. You will not rest from this moment forward until you honor your God-given purpose, calling, and giftings.

From gaming and designing t-shirts to creating art and doing videography, there is an audience for everyone. YES, I'M TALKING TO YOU! If you can produce it, then there's an audience who's willing to support. You may look at it as a hobby, but people are willing to pay for it. Online resources like Etsy and Shopify allow you to open your personalized online shop and sell your products and digital companies like Fiverr allows you to generate income in exchange for your skillset (graphic design, editing, voice overs, etc.). It may take some time to gain a following in these areas, but the more consistent you are, the better you'll do in terms of income.

My husband and I have agreed that our children, by the age of 10, must have their own business with a marketing plan, balance books, and a savings account. After eight years, they will have experience in business and will have options and opportunities available to them. If we are honing and helping them to develop that business and a fiscally responsible mindset, then by the age of 18, they will be light years ahead of the game and already in beast-mode for business, economics, and entrepreneurship.

If you desire to start a business but are not sure how or where to start, think about what you would do for free if money were not an issue, meaning you had all the money you need. Also, think about what comes easy and natural for you to do or a hobby you enjoy. This is a talent and gift that could be monetized into a new stream of income. One of my sisters, Jeanetta Goss of Peacez of Me Art turned her love of completing jigsaw puzzles into a business. She has creatively transformed puzzles into beautiful works of art.

Maybe you don't feel like you have a profitable talent or skillset. You can look at what's irritating you the most, causing you the most pain and anxiety. That can be the area where you need to start your business. This is what Daniel Kane did. He was fed up with having a bulky wallet in his pocket, so he created a streamlined wallet, The Ridge. His frustration led him to an idea, which turned into a multi-million dollar brand.

Whether the business started through a passion or frustration, always be a student of your craft. Learn, develop, and grow. If you're a good cook, what does it take to become great? YouTube, virtual Master Classes, ongoing e-training courses can take you far without having to step foot in a classroom. Leverage the free tools that's at your fingertips.

With access to most of the modern world being a few clicks away, it is now easier than ever to leverage your skillset from home, online, or while on the go using your phone.

2. Rental Income

Rental income is earned when you acquire commercial or residential property and rent it out to someone else. It could be an office building being leased to another business owner, a vacation home turned into an Airbnb, an apartment building unit that is being rented out to multiple tenants, or a home being leased to a family.

The beauty in this stream is that you don't need the full value of the property upfront. There are banks, private investors, and other entities that are willing to loan you money to buy real estate. When successful, you can make thousands of dollars with little or no effort by simply owning a piece of valuable property and renting it out. The income potential is very luring, but you must do a total cost of ownership to get the full picture of profitability. Things like maintenance, legal fees, insurance, and related costs should be considered when deciding.

3. Capital Gains Income

Capital gains are profits generated from the sale of an asset or investment, provided the sale nets you more than the price you originally paid. Nearly any asset you own is a capital asset, whether it's a form of investment or something purchased for personal use (RV, boat, etc.). One of the most common methods of earning capital gains is investing in stocks, bonds, mutual funds, and real estate. These capital assets have proven the test of time and have historically outperformed inflation. Additionally, these investments can pay dividends that can be reinvested for greater returns on your initial investment (compound interest).

4. Interest Income

Interest income is a way to earn money, albeit this stream of income is slow and low on returns. It is the amount paid to you or your business for lending your funds to an institution or individual. As an interest-bearing investor, whether you provide financial backing to a bank, business, or person, the projects or investments you've financed will net you a profit.

A common example of interest income is the interest paid by the bank for depositing AND leaving funds UNTOUCHED in their savings account. The bank will use these deposits to lend money to borrowers. While the bank will earn interest (on average 3-10%) by lending money out, they will also pay interest (national average is a whooping 0.06%) to holders of deposit accounts.

At the end of every month, the account statement will reflect the interest that the bank pays for borrowing the account holder's money.

Other examples of investments that generate interest income are CD's (Certificate of Deposit), money market accounts, stocks, and bonds. Another interest-bearing income means is investing in a 401(k) or 457 plan for retirement.

5. Dividend Income

Dividend income is a form of income you earn by owning shares in a company, commonly known as dividend stocks. Money is earned when the company decides to distribute their earnings as dividends and pay out their profits to shareholders, so if you own stock in a company, you will be paid depending on how many shares of stock you own. For example, if you own 55 shares of stock in a company and that stock pays $4 in annual dividends, you will earn $220 a year just by owning that stock.

In lieu of receiving your dividends, you may have the option to use a dividend reinvestment plan (DRIP) to automatically reinvest your dividends into more shares of stock. This compound method of reinvestment will help you accelerate your profits.

In addition to having a diverse portfolio inclusive of dividend stocks, careful consideration should be given to ensuring you invest in high-quality stocks with a long history of paying dividends. The likelihood of these companies continuing along this profit-sharing path is much greater than the one-offs or inconsistent stocks.

6. Royalty and Licensing Income

Royalty income can be a terrific way to supplement your regular income, and it's a wonderful way to make money from your creative endeavors. Royalty income is received when you license your intellectual property to another person or entity. Simply put, you are the creative genius behind the product, process, or program and you have agreed to allow another person or entity to license it in exchange for payment. The royalty rate is generally set up as a percentage of the sales price per unit sold, but it could also be based on how many times the product has been licensed out (for example, if you license your song for use in commercials, you get paid each time it is played).Books and music are just two examples of perpetual royalty, provided the work is in existence on a platform. The beauty is that you do the work once and collect royalties for a lifetime.

7. Advertising Income

Advertising income is income generated primarily by partnering with companies and allowing their ads on your platform. This could be from social media, blogs, and websites, to name a few outlets. For instance, if your Instagram followers reach more than 100,000 and they consistently respond to your posts, or YouTube channel gets 75,000 views or your blog gets 25,000 visitors, this consistency in traffic attracts the attention of companies who pay influencers to promote their brand on your platform. You have an audience with the people they are trying to reach.

If you have been on YouTube longer than 30 seconds, you undoubtedly have seen advertising income in action. When Gary and I were deep in our bathroom DIY project, YouTube was a go-to for video tutorials. Those five second clips right before the video we wanted to see generate advertising income. Whenever someone clicks on the video and watches that ad, the advertiser pays the video creator money. The more views the video has, the more money the content creator makes from the advertiser.

8. Earned Income

Earned income, which is how most people make their income, refers to any money you generate through working or providing services over time or effort. It can be wages, salaries, tips, commissions, or any other form of compensation. This type of income is one most people understand, in that hours are traded for dollars. But this is also the income category that tend to turn into a trap because it's most familiar, most comfortable, yet the most limiting and might I even say debilitating, as the bulk of time and energy is focused on making money in just this area, eventually robbing some of opportunities to explore and expand their portfolio. Many people attempt to make more money by trading more of their time. If you want to earn more money, most likely the people around you would tell you to work more hours, giving up more time you don't have the luxury to surrender. Anyone who has achieved a level of success and financial independence will tell you that they did not get there by solely working at a job. They strategically used their time and resources to generate more income.

Each of us are allotted 1,440 minutes each day. What separates the rich from the poor, the successful from the marginalized, the producers from the consumers, is how they choose to spend their 1,440 time-currency. Some examples of how to maximize your 1,440 while working as an income earner is becoming a social media influencer, partnering with branded companies, and leveraging life insurance, amongst other things. All these methods focus on maximizing income while minimizing time spent.

Continue to diversify your portfolio with the above-mentioned or other streams of income. Don't limit yourself. The possibilities are endless.

Diversification will help protect your wealth during times of market volatility. If your income comes from just one resource, you risk becoming financially dependent on that one resource, as you are putting all your eggs in one basket and hoping nothing breaks. God forbid something happens like a massive layoff; that could put you in a very vulnerable situation…. financially, emotionally, mentally, physically.

Additional revenue streams are also important because they provide you with more growth opportunities. If one stream runs dry, another can take its place.

TIP

- Don't be afraid to lean on your professional support system and network. A referral can be the difference between landing a deal and generating income right away or continuing the manual search.

PHASE 3

RECONCILE

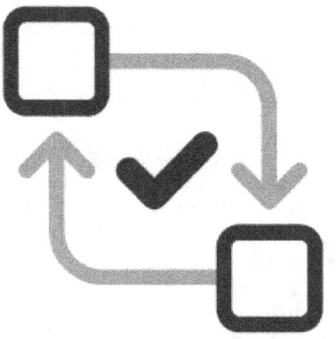

Reconcile · /rĕk′ən-sīl′/[28]

verb

to bring into agreement; harmony; make compatible or consistent:
to cause to become friendly or peaceable again, no longer opposed.

As you enter Reconcile, the goal is symbiotic harmonies between your money and your mind. You will reconcile your finances to remove inconsistencies that bring you to a place free of financial civil war between yourself and your accounts.

As you transition off of this 21-day spending fast, you will develop a plan to maintain what you have gained.

DAY 18

THE POWER OF NO

"Your NO does not require an explanation or justification. "

~C.A. Morris

It's incredibly challenging to live a debt-free life if you're forever the "go-to" ATM for family and friends. From attending a wedding in Tulum, a boy's trip to Vegas, dinner and drinks with friends, to helping a family member who was recently laid off or helping to pay for the funeral of an uncle who didn't have life insurance. And let's not forget about the things you do to soothe or celebrate you. There are plenty of occasions to "protect your peace," including my favorite, a spa and shopping day. This "protecting your peace" mantra has derailed many budgets all in the name of self-care. Therefore, it's important to keep the word no in your vocabulary, not only for others, but for yourself as well.

No. I can't go out to dinner!

No. I can't take that vacation!

No. I don't need another pair of shoes

No. I can't loan you the money

No. I don't need this new car

From the novice saver to the more experienced capitalist, opportunities abound from those closest to you to "invest" in them. Trust me, I know and understand. I cannot count the number of "GoFundMe" projects I've been invited to help support… funerals, mortgage payments, utilities, lace front wigs, weed dispensaries. I allowed my heart strings to be pulled, especially when it came to family. Because I don't like to see my loved ones suffering, I did what I could to help alleviate distress, even if it were to my financial detriment.

After the millionth request to provide humanitarian relief ☺ and having a passive aggressive attitude about giving afterwards, I decided to break out of this toxic cycle. I began to remove emotions from requests to provide "economic stimulus packages." I joke but I was in a bad emotional and financial situation. It was difficult to say no, especially to family. I learned to establish boundaries with my money and mind. Remember this.... As you manage your mind, you will manage your money.

The first time I told a family member no, it hurt me more than it hurt them. I felt guilty, responsible for their pain, and cold-hearted, as many of us are taught that no is a selfish word. I had to reprogram my mindset from having those automatic negative thoughts. Instead of seeing the no as a guilt-ridden answer, I trained my brain to see it as a yes to building a secure financial future. I also saw my no as an opportunity for that person to engage in better planning. I was giving myself permission not to be the 'get-out-of-jail-free card.' The 'no' went beyond giving money but was also a line being drawn in the ground to say I am no longer allowing your lack of planning to become my liability and priority.

My 'no' also began to transcend money. No to people who want to waste my time (time is money). No to people who want to use me as an emotional dumping ground. Do you not realize that misplaced and

116

mismanaged emotions can lead to emotional spending (refer to Day 3)? Learn to set healthy emotional boundaries because it can have a trickle-down effect. If you are not in a good space and place emotionally to have certain conversations, do not answer the phone, do not agree to go out with that person, do not take that meeting. It may end up taxing your budget and your mind.

I believe in you and know that you will come to a crossroads in life where you will confidently say "No, Don't call me," and finally mean it, when you turn down the friend's request for a helping hand, the coworker's request for assistance with a "fire drill" project that was just put on their plate, and even your husband's anticipation that dinner will appear before him 5 minutes after you walk through the door or his honey-do list to be completed within 24 hour. Your 'no' is acknowledging and embracing that you have goals of your own from which you refuse to be deflected any longer.

What's so off and frankly sad is that people are widely celebrated for their 'yes' (they are generous and desire to help), while the 'no' people are often mislabeled and appreciated far less (they are selfish and unkind). We're often taught to put the needs of others above our own, to give instead of take, after all, it is more blessed to give than to receive. For many of us, pleasing others is just hardwired into our brains. At times, a 'yes' can reflect a toxic enabling trait within you which you have not recognized or flat out refuse to accept. You are not a superhero or savior. Your 'yes' is allowing your loved one to continue their self-destructive patterns of behavior and lessening their motivation to change. It's time to cut the umbilical cord, find your voice, empower them to stand on their own and solve their problems.

Don't get me wrong, helping people is a generous, admirable, and noble thing to do—emotionally, spiritually, and even professionally. Balance and boundaries are essential to maintain your plan, priority, path, and peace. Whether you employ softening techniques like "I'm not comfortable with that." "I'd prefer not to." "I'd rather..." "Let's agree to disagree here," "That's a good/nice/interesting plan, but I won't be able to..." or give a firm and flat NO, you must send a clear and powerful message so that the requester clearly understands you will not be providing aid.

You may need to rehearse your 'no's' until you become proficient at it. Scenarios like an indigent family member who has no limits to their requests for money, a friend who always want to go out, a child who puts constant demands on your schedule, a difficult manager who continues loading you with projects, can be the fuel to drive you to practice delivering thoughtful yet deliberate responses to their requests.

These two letters contain enough power to reduce stress, exert control, and maintain your life and finances. When you say no at the right time, you exert your authority to set healthy boundaries, reduce unnecessary stress, and protect your mental and financial health.

TIP

- Before saying yes, ask yourself, "Will it get me closer to my goals?"

If it seems like the offered opportunity might put a drain on your time, money, or mental health, consider turning it down. Remember, you are on a direct path leading to financial freedom and you want to get there as quickly as you can. Don't say yes to anything that might send you on a detour or distract you from your goal.

DAY 19

FINANCIAL DREAM TEAM

"Teamwork is the secret that makes common people achieve uncommon results.

~Ifeanyi Enoch Onyoha

The 1992 U.S. Men's Olympic Basketball Team was some of the most exciting sports I had ever viewed on television. This "Dream Team" consisted of professional players from the NBA. Many have touted that this gathering of GOATs (greatest of all time) was the greatest sports team (not just basketball) to ever be assembled. Watching Michael Jordan, Karl Malone, David Robinson, Patrick Ewing, Magic Johnson, Larry Bird, and others all on one team was mind-blowing in the world of sports. Not only did they beat every opponent by an average of 44 points and take home the gold, but they were also collectively inducted into the U.S. Olympics Hall of Fame. The Dream Team became the standard to meet or beat for all other teams following them.

Now what does Warren Buffett, Oprah Winfrey, Bill Gates, Tyler Perry, the Walton family, and others like them have in common? They applied the same concept to their financial lives. They assembled a dream team to help them manage and protect their wealth. With changing laws and shifts in requirements, a Financial Dream Team has never been more essential. The right team of professional advisors will create a partnership with you to not only achieve your financial goals but to also protect your wealth. Although there are those who can be your mentor or money buddy (accountability partner), here is the starting lineup of your dream team.

Financial Advisor

Personally, the role of Financial Advisor (FA) is the main player on your team. They are like the glue to keeping this team tightly joined together. The FA can help with recommendations for an estate planner, lawyer, accountant, insurance agent, stockbroker, and others.

One of the key responsibilities of the FA is to get an intimate understanding of your financial backstory and where you would like to be. Their job is to get granular with your goals so that they can jointly develop a working plan to achieve your goals and maintain your results. Your FA will also check in with you to monitor your progress with budgeting, managing debt, insurance coverage, building your legacy, taxation, and investments.

When vetting a FA (that was your clue to interview multiple people for the role before deciding on who you will entrust with your financial life), look for one who is not only a fit with your style and function but also look for one who is a Certified Financial Planner, Chartered Financial Analyst or Certified Public Accountant. This credentialed individual has not only gone through extensive training, exams, and work hours to be certified but they are also mandated to function as a fiduciary, meaning they are obligated by law to act in your best interest as they manage your financial assets. Their primary motivation is not self-interest for fees and commissions. And the bonus is that they must have continuing education credits to maintain their credentials, so they will be keeping abreast of the latest laws governing the financial sector.

Tax Accountant

With the complexities of tax regulations and the seeming annual changes, it is imperative that your team is comprised of a highly skilled accountant who will keep you up to date and try to anticipate changes you need to make. Working in tandem with your FA to generate a financial assessment of your portfolio (including reviews of your past records), a worthwhile accountant should be able to provide a holistic current view and future projections of your tax status. Ideally, your research for a Tax Accountant (TA) should center around individuals who are licensed certified public accountants (CPAs).

Estate Attorney

As you continue assembling your dream team, an Estate Attorney (EA) should be commissioned to help you plan for the transitions of life. From formalizing living wills, power of attorney, and beneficiaries to documenting final arrangements, wealth allocations and trust management, the EA is tasked with protecting you, your family, and your assets.

Insurance Agent

The insurance agent is crucial in providing protection to you, your family, and your assets. The insurance agent's job is to find the best policy for your situation. Since your agent will be selling you insurance policies, you may find that an independent agent is the best resource, since he or she won't be tied to one company or product.

TIP

- As your business and wealth grows, don't be afraid to empower others to work on your behalf. Remember, when you hire people because of their skills and experience, let them do their jobs.

DAY 20

~~FAKE IT TIL YOU MAKE IT~~

~~FAITH IT TILL YOU MAKE IT~~

FAITH IT!

"Faith is a choice, not a feeling. It means choosing to trust God
even when life doesn't seem to make sense."
~Dave Willis

"Fake it till you make it!" I'm sure many of you have heard and even said that phrase. Quite a few people swear by this mantra, as it gets them in the game, ready to step up to center stage. I get the concept of what people mean when they say 'fake it,' but sometimes, faking it just isn't going to cut it. Even as a child, there was something about that sentence that always rubbed me the wrong way. In a time and place where you must fight to show up as your authentic self, projecting an air of fakeness can no longer be tolerated.

When life gets a bit stressful or you feel overwhelmed, without a second thought, you may utter "I just need to fake it 'til I make it!" In essence you are saying: "I'm pretending I know what I'm doing, like I have it all together, and it's all good, when in fact, I am actually feeling so overwhelmed and so lost that I'm ready to walk away from it all!" This imposter syndrome (yes, I said what I said) can come because you fear what others think. Or maybe you see being vulnerable as a weakness, so you pretend you are okay, and everything is fine, until you get to where you need to be, all the while, emotionally suffering behind fake smiles and false confidence. Some continue making failed attempts to do it in their own strength, as a 'team of me,' trying to forge forward while working to fend off a total mental meltdown. They push themselves to keep on keeping on, whilst suffering emotionally behind a masked smiles.

Allowing yourself to be vulnerable is an indicator of just how strong you are, as it displays a refreshing rawness, honesty, and transparency to show everything is not ok and that you need to rely on others, especially God. At these moments in life, you need something more than 'faking it' to get you to the 'making/made it' side. Trade in the fake and move into faith.

Now what others may ascribe to is the 'Faith it til you make it' mindset. For me (and for many of you!), my truth and my rock is Jesus Christ, so 'faith it 'til you make it' resonated so strongly with me. During challenging moments (which can feel like years) when your most prevailing thought is to take the path of comfort and convenience and quit, the only thing that helps you get through the storm is faith. Because sometimes you just want to take that highway to heaven and say, "Yo God, I need this, like, last week. Can you make it happen, pronto?" But that microwave manifestation isn't the purpose and plan of faith. This will not teach you the lessons needed nor develop your confidence, patience, and discipline.

At times, you will not understand the purpose, see the path, or like the process but you must trust the plan. You must trust Him even when you can't trace His steps. You must have faith that God will guide you to where you're meant to be. Through prayer, patience, and practice, you will get everything you are believing to manifest for you. When you lean on God as your guide and source, do what is in your power to do, and let go of what's beyond your control, it activates your faith. It not only activates your faith in God but also in yourself... faith that you'll get there... faith that you've got the knowledge, the passion, the capabilities, and the connections to make it happen... faith that you're doing what you can at this very moment to advance... faith that you are prepared to perform.

Faith and positive confessions will help anchor you when challenges try to tell you that it's impossible. Faith will keep pushing you forward when everything around you is telling you to give up. Faith will fuel your dream and desire to go for everything that is for you. Faith will drive you past the haters. Faith will propel you past the naysayers. Faith will have you making boss moves. Faith will put you in a room of influencers that will favor and fund your vision.

I was once a believer of the 'faith it 'til you make it' mantra, because, after all, it takes faith to get you through difficult times and it was better than being fake. The problem with the phrase is that this type of faith is fickled and fleeting; this faith only exists until you make it. The reality is that faith it until you make it is not faith at all. If your faith only lasts during trouble, is it true faith? To me, this statement reads like you just need enough faith until you reach your goal. Then, after you've made it, faith is no longer a necessity. But what happens if you don't make it to your intended destination? What happens if you don't become wealthy?

Faith It!

What happens if your business is not successful? What happens if your investments are not lucrative? You must learn to believe and trust God, independent of the outcome. God calls us to always believe Him.

So, then faithing it says, "I will trust God whether or not I get the millions, whether or not I get everything from my vision board." Faithing it aligns your belief to God's plan, not your wish list. Faithing it focuses on the journey and not the destination. Faithing it will have you believing for things to manifest that benefits more than just you. Faithing it will transform your daily affirmations from:

- o I build a million-dollar financial portfolio that generates perpetual wealth.
- o New streams of income will come to me.
- o I make money effortlessly.

To:

- o I am aligned and at peace with God's plan and purpose.
- o I have unshakable faith in my divine path.
- o I accumulate and build wealth to help others along life's journey.

TIP

- • Instead of planning every aspect of your life, ask God what His plan is is for you.

DAY 21

BUILD A LEGACY

"Every day, create your history; every path you take, you're leaving your legacy.

~Michael Jackson

When planning and working towards your financial freedom, it is my sincere hope that you are considering your financial legacy and building generational wealth. This type of planning is typically considered as people move towards retirement. Leaving a legacy for children, grandchildren, and charities takes deliberate preparation.

Popular families like the Kochs, the Waltons, the Kardashians, or the Trumps are just a few examples of generational wealth. If you consider these and other people and you are struggling to build your savings, then saving for the next generation can be overwhelming. And that is completely understandable!

But you don't have to make a fortune to create wealth that will last. You too can leave a legacy like they have for your own children…and their children…and their children's children. As a wife and mother, I am constantly thinking about leaving a lasting legacy and building generational wealth for our children. However, it is so much more than an inheritance. The legacy Gary and I are working on spans a transference of money and property. In addition to creating a beneficiary IRA and Roth

128

IRA, gifting properties, and insurance, stocks, bonds, and annuities with the children as the beneficiaries, we are most passionate about passing on healthy financial habits, a great money mindset, and an arsenal of tools, techniques and technology that will help them cultivate and maintain an independently wealthy mindset.

Imagine how differently things will turn out as we continue to educate them on personal finance and set up tools to add security to their financial future now. They will be financial forces to be reckoned with by the age of 18.

Think about it. What if your parents taught you about money management? What if they had the financial wherewithal to fund your college education? This one financial act could have had a massive impact on your future. Instead of paying down your student loan debt, you could have been saving for your first home or investing more in your retirement.

Realize the fact that your life is the greatest teaching tool you possess. If your kids were to follow in your financial footsteps, where would that lead them? Where would they be headed? If you do not like the answer, then let's look at some ways of solidifying your footprint to leave a lasting financial impression for the generations to come.

1. Continuous Cash Flow. Whether it's a full-time career or entrepreneurship, have a solid means of providing stable income to fund your savings and investing. Added bonuses from traditional jobs include 401k, penchants, and Health Savings Accounts, which are also means of investing and generational gifting.

2. Insulate this cash flow with additional streams of income. We talked about this extensively on Day 16. Chances are that your full-time employment is not enough to get you to the place of long-term wealth. Having extra money coming in through side gigs can provide you with a needed boost to help reinforce your investment portfolio. Just ensure the additional streams do not disrupt family life and quality of life.

3. Passive Income is essential. This is the wheelhouse of the Buffets and Gates of the world… income earned through investing. You can make this type of money while you sleep at night because you don't have to work for it in the traditional sense. Real estate and investing are two of the best generators of passive income. I love this source of income because your money is making money! Who doesn't love that?! For investing, focus on investing in companies with a high compounding rate of return.

4. Leverage life insurance. Life insurance provides the opportunity to protect your family in the event of your untimely death. Without your income, your children might be forced into less-than-ideal financial circumstances. If you make the effort to invest in life insurance now, then it could prevent financial tragedy for your children. The rule of thumb is to get coverage that is 10 to 12 times your annual income.

5. Be conservative with your spending and aggressive with your savings. In addition to actively watching how you spend your money, make sure you are saving enough, have at least a 6-month emergency fund established, and either reinvest your dividends or put it into savings (retirement plan, IRA, etc.).

6. Invest in Your Child's Education. If college is for your child, be positioned in such a way that neither you nor your child will have to take out a loan to pay for school.

7. Train up a child. In addition to investing in traditional education, invest in teaching your children about money, teaching them about a growth mindset, teaching them how to leverage money as a tool and how to be an expert in wielding their tools so that they won't squander their inheritance when they receive it. With a proper mindset, they will maintain and grow what you've worked so hard to earn and pass on to them. If you are planning to pass on a business to them, have them begin shadowing you and the staff, learning every aspect of the business.

8. Make them work for it. Hear me out. Before receiving their inheritance, require them to take a money management course and develop a wealth management team that includes, at minimum, a financial planner, and a CPA.

9.   Memorialize your legacy. Get everything in writing. Work with an estate planner to create your estate plan and living will. Together with your planner, you create a legally binding document that not only lists your assets but also provides instructions on how your wealth should be allocated and who your beneficiaries are.

10.   Create custodial accounts. Waiting until you are dead and gone is the old school way of operating. By establishing a custodial account for your children, you can make and manage investments for and with your child until they reach a certain age, typically between 18 and 21.

TIP

•   Revisit your estate plan on an annual basis. As your wealth changes or grows, you want to ensure you are including the latest and greatest information and assets.

FINAL WORD

And so it begins!

Congratulations on this epic accomplishment. I know it took some effort to lift and shift your mindset. I'm sure it was a challenge facing the 'enemy within me.' If you're like me in needing to take breaks from the intense work just to catch a breath, IT'S OK. Whether you completed all 21 days or focused on Day 1 for 15 days, you've started and are actively making headway. You're putting the work in and will continue to do so. This time around, you are taking ownership of your destiny.

I invite you to journal your journey using the companion Spending Detox Journal to Freedom (go to 21DaySpendingDetox.com to order). It will contain tools, tips, and assignments (yes, you must put the work in to get a different result). This journal will help you take practical steps to renew your thinking towards money and challenge you to reposition your financial trajectory to have maximum impact.

Now, don't think for one second that I was even perfect or persistent in applying all this information. Prior to my divine disruption, I was one who was into the 'look of riches.' I told myself I deserved the nicer purses, shoes, trips, clothes, and other goods. I worked hard and should enjoy the fruits of my labor. It was not until I had a hard reality check during my time of prayer and meditation when I heard that gentle, still, small voice that asked me one question… "Are you more focused on the appearance of wealth over the assurance of wealth?" WHEW! Yes, it hit me hard, but it was such a loving check to say shift your priorities. Glitz and glam will get me nowhere fast, except the pawn shop to cash in for a needed float.

It took AND continues to take me being deliberate with my decisions. Delayed gratification has become my new bestie. I aim to be intentional with my money matters. Do I get it right every time? NO! Did I hit resistance points, even after making great strides? YES! Yet, I give myself the grace to learn from the opportunity presented and course correct. Time and experience have taught me not to fall back into that old toxic pattern of defining myself from the mistake I made. At the beginning, I had to tell myself aloud, "YOU ARE NOT YOUR MISTAKE. The mistake was an event, a moment in time. Get back up and try again."

You owe it to yourself to keep pressing forward. You've shown up for countless people, now show up for yourself! One day, one step, one moment at a time. Stay the course.

I believe in you and am confident you will make it happen. Whatever you 'it' is, with perseverance and consistency, you will look back and say, "I DID THAT!"

You can purchase the Spending Detox Journal on
www.21DaySpendingDetox.com.

You will be able to download the 21-Day
Spending Detox App *September 2024*.

Sign up at

www.21DaySpendingDetox.com

to receive updates.

REFERENCES

1. Collins English Dictionary – Complete and Unabridged, 12th Edition 2014. (1991, 1994, 1998, 2000, 2003, 2006, 2007, 2009, 2011, 2014). Retrieved December 20, 2021, from https://www.thefreedictionary.com/reflect

2. 3 Practical Tips for Changing the Way You Think About Money by Robert M. Gouge © 2019. Retrieved November 19, 2021. https://www.lifehack.org/articles/money/3-practical-tips-for-changing-the-way-you-think-about-money.html

3. Five Myths About the Lottery by George Loewenstein. © 2019. Retrieved January 1, 2022. https://www.washingtonpost.com/outlook/five-myths/five-myths-about-the-lottery/2019/12/27/742b9662-2664-11ea-ad73-2fd294520e97_story.html

4. How Clutter Affects Our Mental Health by Kristen Fuller MD. © 2021. Retrieved January 2, 2022. https://verywellmind.com/decluttering-our-house-to-cleanse-our-minds-510511

5. What the Average American Woman's Closet is Worth by Glamour. © 2016. Retrieved January 2, 2022. https://www.huffpost.com/entry/average-spent-on-clothes_b_7707112/amp

6. How Much Time Do We Spend Searching for Things by IKEA. © 2017. Retrieved January 1, 2022. https://www.ikea.com/es/en/ideas/how-much-time-do-we-spend-searching-for-things-around-the-home-pubec2a8ae0

7. Lost and Found by PRNewsWire. © 2017. Retrieved January 2, 2022. https://www.prnewswire.com/news-releases/lost-and-found-the-average-american-spends-25-days-each-year-looking-for-lost-items-collectively-costing-us-households-27-billion-annually-in-replacement-costs-300449305.html

8. How to Avoid Financial Infidelity in Your Relationship by Christopher Sonzogni. © 2021. Retrieved January 4, 2022. https://www.investopedia.com/how-to-avoid-financial-infidelity-in-your-relationship-4687135

9. Financial Infidelity by Jini Thornton. © 2015. Retrieved December 15, 2021. https://6e553e7c-f697-46d7-879f-e6cf8c328338.filesusr.com/ugd/b87d69_00f9452fb8004628ba95b42a3ecfc9d3.pdf

10. Ibid #12

11. American Heritage® Dictionary of the English Language, Fifth Edition. Copyright © 2016 by Houghton Mifflin Harcourt Publishing Company. Published by Houghton Mifflin Harcourt Publishing Company. All rights reserved.). Retrieved December 20, 2021, from https://www.thefreedictionary.com/redirect

12. National Resources Defense Council, Food Waste, © 2021 by NRDC. Retrieved on December 29, 2021, from https://www.nrdc.org/food-waste

13. What Does the Bible Say About Money by Katie Jones. © 2021. Retrieved January 4, 2022. https://agapeinvests.com/over-100-bible-verses-about-money/

14. The Complex Story of American Debt by The Pew Charitable Trusts. © 2015. Retrieved January 4, 2022.
https://pewtrusts.org/-/media/assets/2015/07/reach-of-debt-report-artfinal.pdf

15. 7 Ways Debt is Bad for Your Health by Amanda MacMillan and Mia Taylor. © 2021. Retrieved January 4, 2022.
https://www.health.com/conditions/stress/ways-debt-is-bad-for-your-health

16. Debt-to-Income Ratio Calculator by Dave Ramsey. © 2021. Retrieved January 2, 2022.
https://www.ramseysolutions.com/debt/debt-to-income-ratio-calculator?utm_source=google&utm_id=go_cmp-12426289913_adg-120037789884_ad-501329170022_kwd-330561203435_dev-m_ext-_prd-_mca-_sig-Cj0KCQiAoNWOBhCwARIsAAiHnEhqeVb_RdtxNsezMwsUqPiBnPfKAI4mHM4emomgpUtpiMQ370fOsL0aAi9vEALw_wcB&gclid=Cj0KCQiAoNWOBhCwARIsAAiHnEhqeVb_RdtxNsezMwsUqPiBnPfKAI4mHM4emomgpUtpiMQ370fOsL0aAi9vEALw_wcB

17. 84 YouTube Statistics You Can't Ignore in 2022 by Sarika from InVideo. © 2022. Retrieved July 24, 2022.
https://invideo.io/blog/youtube-statistics/#:~:text=YouTube%20has%202%20billion%20active%20users%20every%20month,22%2C000%20of%20them%20have%20crossed%201%20million%20subscribers.

18. The Definitive Guide to Saving Money by Going Green by The Ascent Staff. © 2019. Retrieved December 2021. https://www.fool.com/the-ascent/research/definitive-guide-money-going-green/

19. Mind the Workplace by Mental Health America. © 2021. Retrieved February 12, 2022. https://mhanational.org/sites/default/files/Mind%20the%20Workplace%20-%20MHA%20Workplace%20Health%20Survey%202021%202.12.21.pdf

20. Work Depression: How to Take Care of Your Mental Health on the Job by Sara Lindberg. © 2021. Retrieved February 12, 2022. https://www.healthline.com/health/depression/work-depression

21. Median Income by State by Ward Williams. © 2021. Retrieved February 12, 2022. https://www.investopedia.com/median-income-by-state-5070640

22. Ibid 21

23. Forbes World's Billionaires List by Kerry Dolan. © 2022. Retrieved February 26, 2022. https://www.forbes.com/billionaires/

24. Key findings about U.S. immigrants by Pew Research Center. © 2020. Retrieved February 16, 2022. https://www.pewresearch.org/fact-tank/2020/08/20/key-findings-about-u-s-immigrants/

25. World's Wealth Hits Half a Quadrillion Dollars by Ollie Williams. © 2021. Retrieved February 16, 2022.

https://www.forbes.com/sites/oliverwilliams1/2021/06/10/world
s-wealth-hits-half-a-quadrillion-dollars/?sh=44c29ca6309d

26. Ibid 23

27. 7 Income Streams of Millionaires by Dan Lok. © 2021.
    Retrieved February 26, 2022. https://danlok.com/7-income-
    streams-of-
    millionaires/#:~:text=The%20reason%20why%20millionaires%
    20are%20able%20to%20generate,the%20middle%20class%2C
    %20only%20have%20one%20income%20stream.

28. Random House Kernerman Webster's College Dictionary, © 20
    10 K Dictionaries Ltd. Copyright 2005, 1997, 1991 by Random
    House, Inc. All rights reserved. Retrieved December 20, 2021,
    from https://www.thefreedictionary.com/reconcile

BIOGRAPHY

WIFE, MOTHER, ENTREPRENEUR, AND AUTHOR, CHARITY IS PASSIONATE ABOUT HELPING PEOPLE REALIZE AND REACH THEIR GREATEST POTENTIAL.

Charity is a dynamic teacher who has a gifted ability to communicate with clarity, simplicity, revelation, and passion. She pulls from her experiences and uses humor to help keep her audience actively engaged, entertained, and edified. She has conducted trainings, seminars, workshops, and taught classes in the public and private sector.

As a communicator, she has authored books to help people maximize living, with the latest being 21-Day Spending Detox. She holds a B.A. in Psychology and an A.A. in French from Indiana University Northwest. In 2009, she also graduated from the Joseph Business School. Charity's entrepreneurial gifts manifested as she started her own publishing company, Scribe Publications as well as an merchandising company, Grace Gear.

Charity is the wife of Gary Morris. To their beautiful union, they have four amazing children and reside in Georgia.

If you would like to book Charity to speak at your conference, service, or event, please email booking@charitymorris.com